What is Marriage, Really?

Publication made possible by the

WHAT IS MARRIAGE, REALLY?

From Two Marriage Sermons
On Hebrews 13:4 and Ephesians 5:22–33

By MARTIN LUTHER

Translated by
Holger Sonntag

Edited and Arranged by
Paul Strawn

Lutheran Press
Minneapolis

Lutheran Press, Minneapolis 55432

Printed in the United States of America.

1st Edition

ISBN 978-0-9845351-3-2

Library of Congress Control Number: 2014931135

Book design by Scott Krieger
Cover design by Roxanne Johnson
Cover photography by Alex Nelson
@ http://www.flickr.com/photos/morrowless/

Table of Contents

	Foreword	7
1	*God's Gift to Us*	11
2	*Without Unique Appearance*	15
3	*A Spouse is Truly a Gift*	21
4	*Marriage Does Not Eliminate Temptation*	25
5	*Nor Remove Ignorance of God's Word*	29
6	*Nor Create Perfect Love*	33
7	*Nor Destroy Sinful Desires*	37
8	*Without the Word Marriage Disintegrates*	41
9	*So Why Even Get Married?*	43
10	*Marriage is Purified by God's Word*	49
11	*So Marriage is to be Honored*	53
12	*It is Like Christ's Spiritual Marriage to the Church*	57
13	*As is the Christian Marriage*	63
14	*Which the World Does Not Grasp*	67
15	*The Christian's Spiritual Marriage is Glorious*	73
16	*For the Church is the Bride of Christ*	79
17	*The Christian's Spiritual Marriage Shapes Marriage*	85
	Afterword	89

Foreword

As this brief work on marriage goes to press, the general acceptance of the uniqueness and desirability of a state-established and protected life-long union between a man and a woman seems to be in significant decline. Cohabitation apparently has become the norm as reportedly almost 75 percent of women under the age of thirty in the United States have lived with a partner outside of marriage. The average age of men and women who do get married continues to climb, in 2013 the numbers being 26.5 years for women and 28.5 for men—an all time high. The divorce rate, on the other hand, is down from an all time high of 50% in the 1980's but is still over 40%. Additionally, homosexual marriage continues to gain greater acceptance both socially and legally. The state of Minnesota, for example, recently joined 13 other states in opening marriage to homosexuals while the Supreme Court of the United States has struck down a California law prohibiting same-sex marriages. In Europe, 22 of 51 countries currently recognize some sort of same-sex partnership.

What has happened to marriage? Perhaps the simplest answer is that people have forgotten, or have never learned, what marriage truly is. Growing up in an age of cohabitation, divorce and homosexuality, how could they be expected to know? Somewhat surprisingly, in Martin

Luther's day—the 16th century—the people of Europe found themselves struggling with the concept of marriage as well. At that time, the ideal life was seen to be a life without any type of sexual relations at all. The celibate life of the monk and the nun was lauded, while marriage was viewed as a life of sinful desire and lust. And back then, as now, children were an issue, with their birth not being heralded as good news, but simply as an outcome, a necessity of the marital life, and presenting another mouth to feed. Surprisingly, laws of inheritance and other social pressures presented cohabitation as a viable and desirable option then as now.

So the text of this work. It is a compilation of two sermons which Luther preached on marriage, one on Hebrews 13:4 and the other on Ephesians 5:22-33. That first appeared together as a single publication in 1536. Here Luther lays down three basic principles for a good and happy marriage. The first is to recognize that marriage is not created by man, but by God. A second is that marriage is meant for man's benefit, for his comfort and well-being. The third: Marriage takes place within the greater context of another marriage, that is, the marriage of Christ and his Church. The Afterword contains a detailed account of the publication history of this work, along with the social and theological context in which it should be understood.

Thanks are due to Nathan and Sheila Rinne, Sue Ulfeng, and my wife Kristi who read rough drafts of this work and offered many helpful suggestions for its improvement. Thanks also are due to the Confessional Lutheran Education Foundation for providing significant financial support toward its printing. Roxanne Johnson (formerly Nelson) once again did a wonderful job on the cover, and here special mention must also be given to Scott Krieger. He has worked tirelessly on all of the books of this series, selflessly embracing the tedium of obscurities such as call-out box placement and header and footer format. Without his efforts, these works would have never made it to press, nor would the soon-to-be released electronic editions ever have been made available! For his continuing labors I am nothing but grateful and express my most humble and heartfelt thanks!

Paul Strawn

1

God's Gift to Us

I have often preached and written about the institution of marriage and the married life. Now I want to say a few things in its honor.

Marriage is one of the most necessary topics to be preached in the church. All Christians should know what marriage is.

The church is Christ's holy people

Although marriage is the most common institution of human life, it is, in fact, the most honorable one. All other institutions exist and are sustained by marriage.

This is why the holy apostles write about marriage and diligently admonish us concerning marriage in their letters (e.g., in 1 Cor. 7; Eph. 5; Col. 3; 1 Peter 3). In Hebrews 13, for example, the Apostle Paul states:

> *Let marriage be held in honor by all, and the marriage bed be kept undefiled. Yet God will judge the fornicators and adulterers.*

In this verse the apostle is not addressing all people everywhere. Instead, he is teaching baptized Christians what they are to think about marriage.

Christians should not think that marriage is insignificant. They should certainly not treat marriage in a superficial or shameful way. This is what the world does now and has always done.

But up until now, the same thing was happening within Christianity! Virginity was greatly praised as the ideal, while marriage was disparaged as utterly worthless! By doing such a thing, it was thought that somehow the world would be made chaste. Instead, the world has simply become filled with the disgrace of fornication.

Christians should not disparage marriage. Rather, they should learn to honor and praise marriage as a Christian and blessed institution of human life.

Christians should also keep the institution of marriage free from fornication and wickedness. This is what the apostle calls *holding marriage in honor and keeping the marriage bed undefiled.*

But what else is meant by these words? The first thing is that everyone should be convinced of the fact that God himself has ordained and established the institution of marriage and all similar institutions. So understandably the most-desired skill of married life is this: To learn to think of marriage according to the honor given it by God.

What is that honor? That God himself established the institution of marriage and speaks of it in his Word.

But marriage appears to be a common every-day experience. Each Christian thinks he can figure it out for himself.

Who needs a teacher for marriage? What Christian does not know that the institution of marriage was established by God in the Garden of Eden? That marriage was confirmed by God outside of Eden? Moses tells us all about it in Genesis 1, 2 and 9!

Who needs a teacher for marriage?

I myself have read these passages frequently and have even memorized them. Still, this most-desired skill of married life I have not yet mastered. Even though I am an old doctor of theology, I must not be ashamed to learn about marriage daily.

The words of Scripture about marriage are learned quickly. There it states plainly that marriage is an institution established by God.

Yet the main thing here is this skill to which I am referring in my own marriage and all others: We should be certain, and not doubt that the institution of marriage has been created, ordained and established by God. In fact, we should consider this institution to be God's gift to mankind.

---

1. What is the most common institution of human life?

2. Why do the apostles write about marriage?
3. What should Christians learn to do in view of marriage?
4. From what should the institution of marriage be kept free?
5. What honor does God give marriage?
6. In view of marriage, of what should the Christian be certain?

2

Without Unique Appearance

The world in its madness, of course, and man with his reason does not seriously believe that marriage is ordained and established by God. The common man thinks that marriage happens by coincidence. That whether we marry this person or that is simply a matter of chance. Like when we run into a person on the street.

This is why the institution of marriage seems to have become nothing more than a foolish game. This is why people talk about marriage with such contempt.

Why? They think of and evaluate marriage only on the basis of its external appearance.

Admittedly, when you look at the two alternatives—marriage and fornication[1]—they appear to be identical ways of living. In fact, they look so similar that there is no difference when it comes to living and sleeping together.

It is no wonder that it is so difficult to master the skill of knowing how to distinguish between marriage and fornication. If it were not so hard, a husband would always be able to say: "God himself has given me my wife in order for me to live with her." Likewise a wife would be able to say: "God himself has given my husband to me. With him I should share my food and bed."

Marriage is to be praised and extolled as much as possible

Above all, this should be diligently taught among the people: The institution of marriage is to be praised and extolled as much as possible! Why? Marriage has become utterly corrupted by unspiritual monks and papal hacks who judge it only according to its external appearance. Consequently they consider marriage to be no different from any other unholy way of life.

Such a determination was a result of the fact they themselves led the same kind of unholy life. Even to the point of drowning in it. This made them unable to think or say anything honorable or holy about marriage. What is more, the best among them burdened the consciences of those in marriage with their bonds and fetters, telling them how they should go about fulfilling their conjugal duties.

---

[1] Fornication is usually considered to be having sexual intercourse before marriage. It is, in other words, a committing of adultery against a future spouse.

A Christian, however, should be able to distinguish clearly between the married and the unmarried life. How? By God's Word.

God attached his Word to the institution of marriage when he said in Gen. 1:27-28: "God created male and female, and gave Eve to Adam. He blessed them saying: 'Be fruitful and multiply'."

This blessing was renewed later in Gen. 9:1, 7. Then there is also Gen. 2:18, 24, where it says: "It is not good for man to be alone. I will make a helper for him who will stand by him…This is why a man will leave his father and mother and cling to his wife. And two will be one flesh."

Matthew 19:6 states: "What God has joined let man not separate." This is the jewel that makes marriage into something honorable. Marriage is a divine work and institution. Without this Word, the institution of marriage would be an unholy way of life and not what it truly is. Instead, marriage is truly noble for in it the Word itself can be seen to shine.

God attached his Word to the institution of marriage

Consider this example. When a murderer kills someone, the act itself looks exactly the same as when someone is executed according to the sentence of a judge.

It is for this reason it has long been held that a judge has a perilous duty. In fact, this one duty of a judge has in the past been described as so horrible that no one could carry it out with a good conscience.

Consequently the sword of the government became dull and rusty. People were scandalized by the death penalty.

Understandably, many fine, honorable judges fled when they were called to decide a capital case—rather than have anything to do with this horrible work!

This and other such errors occur when we consider one's place and duty in society by itself, apart from God's Word. For when a murderer kills someone, he does not do the right thing. He has neither a command to do so nor God's Word. In fact, the murderer acts against God's Word and commandment, which reads: "You shall not kill." This is why his murder is utter darkness, hell, and death.

However, when the government kills someone, it has God's Word and command on its side. This is why the judge or executioner does not use the sword. God does it.

Here the sword shines as if it were in the hand of an angel, even as if it were in God's hand. This happens by the Word which commands evil to be punished, and good to be protected and defended. And just as a murderer sins when he kills, because he is forbidden to do this, so the judge sins when he does not kill, because he is commanded to kill, Rom. 13:4.

Here is another example. When a burglar breaks into someone's house and steals something, then this work is very similar to that of a judge or other government official who goes about imposing fines on citizens or collecting from them assets pledged as securities.

And yet, there is a big difference between the two. The judge does so lawfully, as the one who should take it. He has the holy hands of God. For God's Word says to him: You shall punish injustice and promote and administer justice.

The burglar has neither a commandment nor the law

on his side, telling him to take what belongs to another. In fact, God has forbidden him to do this: "You shall not steal." This is why the burglar has utterly devilish, accursed hands by which he grabs what is not his.

These two examples shed light on marriage. For when two people, a man and a woman, live together in an unholy way, it looks just like the married life. They help one another getting dressed. They walk and work together. They are just like a married couple when it comes to sleeping and eating. You cannot distinguish between how they are living and the married life based on reason.

In marriage, however, God is present with his Word. God blesses and sanctifies marriage, saying: "When you live with your wife, sleeping and eating with her, it is not the same kind of life that fornicators have together. Rather, it is a holy life together. It is ordained and instituted by God himself."

In marriage, God is present with his Word

And that other life? A life of fornication is forbidden by God. So in Hebrews and in the Ten Commandments God says: "You shall not commit adultery or covet your neighbor's wife."

---

1. What does the world think of marriage?
2. How do people think of and evaluate marriage?
3. Is it difficult to distinguish between marriage and fornication?
4. How is such a distinction made?

5. What makes marriage a divine work and institution?

6. So why is marriage a holy life?

3

A Spouse is Truly a Gift

To talk about the institution of marriage in a Christian way means to praise its most exalted characteristic: God's Word is attached to it. In fact, God's Word is written on each spouse, so that they might look at each other as if they were the only two people on earth.

When this is understood, then no king wearing his crown jewels—in fact, not even the sun—will shine more beautifully than your spouse. For in marriage you have the Word by which God promises and gives this woman or man to you as a gift.

What does the Word say but "This one shall be your

husband. This one shall be your wife. I am well pleased with this! All the angels and creatures rejoice and are glad in it."

Would that everyone thought this way every day! Would that all spouses said: "I am certain that the fact that I sit and live here with my spouse is pleasing to God. For God himself instituted and ordained marriage and commands me to so live in marriage by his Word." This Word of God comforts spouses and creates clear consciences.

Yet those who live together without marriage cannot have such clear consciences. They do not have God's commandment. In fact, they act against God's Word and live together, not in God's name, but in the devil's name.

This Word of God comforts spouses and creates clear consciences

So the ability always to view a marriage as God's doing is a desirable skill which few master. Although I would love to do so, I myself have not mastered it. Longstanding custom causes me again and again not to look to the Word of God concerning marriage, but solely to its outward appearance.

True enough, our flesh is full of evil lusts which entice us to sin. Yet we must not give in to them. Nor must we evaluate the institution of marriage according to them.

Rather, when you hold God's Word up to marriage and consider how it blesses and adorns marriage, you will be sustained and comforted. And marriage itself will become a holy institution for you.

Marriage suffers violence and injustice when it is called merely a worldly institution; especially since other institutions—such as the papacy and monasticism—are considered to be spiritual in nature. Perhaps this is because the devil—their god and founder—is also a spirit. He thought them up and founded them.

For where is a single letter in Scripture about this: That a monk should wear a black or white cowl? That he should follow a specifically prescribed order of life? Eat this and not that?

Yet the institution of marriage is mentioned in Scripture almost at its very beginning. There it is written that God created a male and a female and gave them to one another. He commanded them to be fruitful, beget children, etc.

Now, the institution of marriage has the Word of God. In fact, it is set in God's Word like a jewel is mounted on a ring. This is how marriage is sanctified in the Word and by the Word. You should, therefore, justly respect it greatly and consider it to be a divine institution. In this way, every husband or wife will be safe and certain that he or she is living in a God-pleasing fashion. And that God approves that he or she is not living outside of, but inside of marriage according to God's Word and blessing and will.

What is more, this Word of God is necessary for the sake of conscience. The conscience should not suffer because you fully participate in marriage. For God has created and ordained marriage, and is well pleased by it.

This Word of God also strives against the devil

This Word of God also strives against the devil. For those who think about marriage but are not married, think that it is a life of lustful desires and good times. Such people have not yet tasted or experienced what God's Word is and what the power of God's blessing is.

According to their unchaste thoughts, they only seek to satisfy their desires and have a good time. Yet later, when they are in marriage and find it to be different than they thought it would be, they do not know how to accept this. Why? They do not see or respect any Word of God in it.

---

1. How do we talk about marriage in a Christian way?
2. According to the Word of God, what is a spouse?
3. How does marriage suffer violence and injustice?
4. How is marriage set in God's Word?
5. Which Word of God is necessary for the sake of conscience?

4

Marriage Does Not Eliminate Temptation

When you consider the institution of marriage rightly—how God's Word shines above your spouse's head—the devil will certainly attack you from all sides. He will tempt you in every way possible.

First, there will be a loss of desire for your spouse. You will feel that you've had enough of him or her; that you do not want to remain united with your spouse for long.

Thus your initial desire changes into unwillingness. For the devil cannot stand that spouses remain on friendly terms and united with each another.

So this is why God tolerates the desire which the bride

and the bridegroom have for one another. He must think something like: "I must dupe these fools. For if it were not for desire, you could not get anyone to enter the married life."

The devil is the sworn enemy of the institution of marriage, as he is of all of God's Word and works. The devil hinders and disturbs marriage whenever he can.

He creates stubbornness between husband and wife. They then become impatient with and bitter toward each other. Desire changes into unwillingness, and joy gives way to anger and sorrow.

Those who do not have the grace of contemplating and believing God's Word experience this daily. This is why it says in Sirach 25:1 that there are three beautiful things which please both God and man: 1. When brothers are in agreement; 2. When neighbors love one another; and 3. When husband and wife live in harmony.

The devil is the sworn enemy of the institution of marriage

Why are these three things praised so highly? Because brothers seldom live in peace and unity. The same can be said of neighbors who live next to each other on friendly terms to the extent that one is able to trust the other and expect the best from him. And it is equally rare for spouses to live together in love and harmony.

If you consider this only on the basis of external appearances, you will think: "Well, what's so hard about being friendly to your neighbor? Loving to your spouse? And united with your brothers? If brothers cannot be united, who can be?"

All that is needed is a small inheritance that is to be divided among them. How quickly does one brother betray the other? How often does one brother become another's deadly enemy rather than give him anything from an inheritance?

In the same way also, sisters argue over trivial matters. And neighbors do so as well. How often is one neighbor unfaithful and deceitful to another for the sake of a little thing; perhaps something as insignificant as a chicken?

Similarly, no one experiences alienation from another faster than a husband and wife! A single word spoken flippantly or jokingly can cause it to happen. Such a word cuts right to the heart and simply cannot be forgotten.

No one experiences alienation from another faster than a husband and wife!

The result? Both spouses spew forth fire and brimstone at each other from their hearts.

Why does this happen? Satan is not pleased with peace or unity. And when spouses are not united, what joy or goodness can there be?

This is why you should be well armed against the devil, who is the enemy of marriage and begrudges peace and unity. Resist him and beat him back with God's Word, saying in the face of temptations:

> "No matter what the devil's temptations are, marriage is nevertheless a divine institution of human life. God himself has placed me into marriage. Everything might not be as it is supposed to be in my marriage. I need

patience. I am not supposed or willing to throw away or despise the institution of marriage on account of trouble. Just because not everything within this institution is right, does not mean marriage itself is evil. Things can't always be so pure that it seems like innocent doves have chosen them."

This is also why people say about spouses that get along: It is a special grace and rarely turns out so well.

---

1. Why does the devil attack the person who is married?
2. How does the devil attack?
3. What are the three things that please both God and man?
4. What can quickly cause alienation between a husband and wife?
5. Who is the ultimate cause of such strife in marriage?
6. How is the devil resisted in marriage?

5

Nor Remove Ignorance of God's Word

So let's be honest. It truly is no wonder when spouses do not get along.

Why? They do not understand how the institution of marriage is described by God's Word.

If a married couple could see how in God's Word they are clothed in such bright splendor and radiance, they would not get angry so quickly—even when everything in their marriage is not as sweet as honey.

Rather, they would think that God has caused marriage to be this way, "putting some salt on the roast," so to speak. Why? To increase their appetite for God's Word.

Therefore, if some anger or disgust rears its head, they can subdue it all the more easily. How? By thinking: "Here I have God's Word with which God has adorned and blessed this institution for me. I should desire this adornment rather than destroying this treasure by my unwillingness or anything else. I should yearn for this blessing rather than let something make me no longer love my spouse whom God has given me."

This turns marriage into a hell

This is the one way in which the devil attempts to stir up all sorts of unwillingness and disunity in marriage so that one spouse becomes the other's sworn enemy. This turns marriage into a hell and the devil rejoices.

For do not even think that the devil or the world delights in or desires love and harmony. But God and the Holy Spirit are well pleased with it and rejoice in it.

This is why both St. Paul and St. Peter admonish spouses when they argue to reconcile and come together again (cf. 1 Cor. 7:11) lest their prayer be hindered (cf. 1 Peter 3:7). For the apostles certainly knew how the devil sows his seeds among spouses so that, even among Christians, marriages are rarely without anger and a lack of enthusiasm. Paul and Peter wished to comfort spouses and restore them to peace by the Word.

But this is how it goes: If you are not married, you think that once you are, there will always be laughter and good times. You cannot imagine ever saying a word that might hurt your spouse. You are confident that you will avoid any pitfalls.

At the same time, you think marriage is something that just happens. Or that marriage is something you have invented yourself.

This is wrong. Marriage is God's institution and order.

So this is why marriage must be assaulted by the devil. If you enter into this institution, you enter into a real monastery that is full of temptation.

So go ahead and choose a wife according to your wish. Let her be as pious, rich, beautiful, and friendly as possible. You will still have to work diligently to love her and maintain your friendship with her. For you cannot make this happen.

Marriage is God's institution and order

Besides, you have a formidable foe in your home who is called the devil. He wholeheartedly is displeased when he sees that all things are going well.

Rather, it would give the devil great pleasure if a husband and wife were constantly grumbling and mumbling against one another. Even better: If chairs, benches, and tables were being constantly thrown back and forth!

Then the devil would rejoice! For he would love to see the institution of marriage totally disappear from the face of the earth and to have nothing good ever come out of it. The devil does everything in his power—being the destroyer of God's works and order which he is—to accomplish his goal.

This is why you must not look at the married life as being full of temptation and sorrow. Rather, you must look at marriage according to the Word of God by which it is adorned and in which it is set like a gem.

The Word of God will certainly turn the bitter wormwood of marriage into honey. And turn sorrow once more into gladness.

---

1. So why do spouses not get along with each other?
2. How can anger or disgust in marriage be subdued?
3. In what are God and the Holy Spirit pleased and rejoice?
4. Is marriage something that just happens?
5. Who is the formidable foe to marriage?
6. How must the Christian look at marriage?

6

Nor Create Perfect Love

Realize that after you are married the devil will tempt you with adventurous curiosity and forbidden lust. For you will not be perfectly chaste unless you have a special grace from God.

You will not perfectly love your wife. As a result, from time to time other thoughts will enter your mind, suggesting that another woman is prettier and lovelier than your wife.

In the same way also, your wife will not perfectly love you. Consequently, some other man may turn her head.

"What? May God protect me," you say, "should I not

love my wife!" "Should I become fed up with my husband? May God protect me too!"

Your wife will not perfectly love you

Yet you be watchful as well! Even though you might be chaste, you nonetheless will feel such temptations in your heart, stirred up by your flesh and inspired by the devil—especially if you want to be a Christian.

This is why you here must once more be armed with God's Word. It tells you: "This is your flesh and your bone given and ordained to you from God." By this Word, she is adorned in sheer purple and pieces of gold and precious stones, above all other women on earth. You will not be able to choose or select a better one.

In this way, you can fend off adventurous curiosity and resist the devil so that no other woman becomes lovelier or more desirable than your wife—even if she is homely, obstinate, odd, and unfriendly. Otherwise, if you follow your thoughts and the lures of the devil—making all others look prettier and lovelier than your wife—you have already spoiled such a treasure and adornment together with God's blessing and pleasure.

The result will be complaining on both sides: "The devil misled me to the wrong husband or wife!" "May all those be cursed who brought us together with their advice and schemes!" "If I only had that other woman or that other man! He or she is so friendly and so nice!" In such a way, evil desires will indeed strike, just as the poets write that love rages and raves wildly.

Therefore, let everyone see to it that he may abide by

God's Word and look at his spouse according to it. According to the Word of God, your spouse is clad in the most beautiful jewels put on by God. If you keep this Word before you and always see your reflection in it, your bed, your food, your room, your house, and everything about your wife will become pure gold for you.

This is why you hear God himself say to you: "You shall be your wife's husband. And you, wife, should stand by this husband of yours." This is how God has ordained it.

If you look at your marriage like this and regard it as so precious and priceless, nobody else's wife will please you as much as your own wife. For the Word will not allow it.

Even if you think that some other woman's words or gestures are most kind and beautiful, she is nonetheless—in comparison to your wife—totally ugly in your eyes. For in her you do not find the adornment, which is God's Word. Yet your wife is the prettiest and loveliest for you because she is the one whom God himself has adorned with his dear Word.

Yet, as I have said, it takes the greatest skill to consider this institution according to God's Word. God's Word alone creates a love of marriage and love between spouses. God's Word alone takes away all unwillingness, anger, and impatience.

God's Word alone creates a love of marriage

And if any of these rear their head, they must nevertheless perish and drown as in a deep sea. For the Word of God is a powerful and holy thing. It makes all other things holy if it is recognized and grasped.

1. Can a person perfectly love his or her spouse?
2. What is the source of temptation in the heart?
3. With what should the Christian be armed?
4. Why should the Christian regard their marriage as precious?
5. What alone creates a love of marriage?

7

Nor Destroy Sinful Desires

So what are we lacking? We are unable to have the Word of God always before us. We are often rushed into forgetting it.

And it would be good if we, when we feel tempted, turned quickly back to the Word of God before we let ourselves be overcome by temptation. For it is impossible not to feel and not to be tempted.

The devil is relentless. Wherever he sees people clinging to God's Word, he seeks all kinds of ways and means to remove that Word from before our eyes and to cause us to gawk and gape elsewhere.

Once the devil has accomplished this, he also soon succeeds in making the heart bitter with disgust or impatience. He then inflames it with disorderly desires. Soon, every man or woman will seem prettier, friendlier, more pleasing and better to you than your spouse.

This is why you can see so many fools who have the prettiest and best wives but who attach themselves to shameful, loose, repulsive shrews and hags. Such a thing happens because they do not have the Word of God and because they do not consider marriage to be anything other than an unchaste way of life.

We quickly grow tired of whatever God gives us

Moreover, our flesh is dangerously curious. By nature we are gluttons. We quickly grow tired of whatever God gives us—even if he were to give us everything on earth!

Unless we cling to God's Word, this defect will remain with us. The devil builds on this defect. He blinds people so that they do not see what a precious treasure they have in God's Word. That Word portrays and gives to each her husband or his wife. It also adorns them most gloriously, blessing them, and sanctifying them.

Why? So that there is no reason to look for a different man or woman. For if you do this, you have already committed adultery, as Christ says in Matth. 5:28.

Now, this is also what the holy apostle wishes to teach in Hebrews, as he admonishes Christians to learn to consider the institution of marriage according to God's Word. This is why they should hold this institution near and dear. This is why they should keep the marriage bed pure and undefiled.

For this is, he says, what God wants from you.

However, if you will improve on marriage or change it—as the pope has done with his dear monks and nuns—God will not let you remain without punishment. Papists and Pagans as well are unable to preach properly about marriage. In fact, among them it is considered to be a carnal and worldly institution. They have turned marriage into something that is despised and hated.

They have turned marriage into something that is despised and hated

In comparison to the falsely praised spiritual institutions, marriage had to become something rancid. No one was able to receive any comfort from, or joy out of marriage—although these would be the most necessary aspects of marriage to impress on the conscience!

Now, the apostle says: "Let the married life be honored, and let the marital bed be kept undefiled." These two points he posits over against the two temptations discussed above, namely: 1) That our flesh is full of destructive desires and 2) that both carnal curiosity and gluttony are strong in us. As a result, disgust drives me here, curiosity there, evil desire elsewhere.

So the phrase "let the marital bed be kept undefiled" is obviously not about washing bedroom linens. Rather this impurity and these stains in the marital bed are nothing other than fornication and adultery, as the apostle himself explains later on in Hebrews. These are the real shameful spots that defile, stain, and dishonor the marital bed.

1. So what do spouses in a marriage lack?

2. What are we to do in marriage when tempted?

3. What is the result of being by nature gluttons?

4. Why does the Christian hold the institution of marriage near and dear?

5. Is the phrase "let the marital bed be kept undefiled" about washing sheets?

8

Without the Word Marriage Disintegrates

No matter how good they pretend to be before the world, those who live together without being married, in fornication, consider marriage to be nothing. The same thing is done by those who are married but commit adultery against God's command and order.

In general, all who look at marriage as if it were something that occurs by happenstance and by chance do violence to it. For they do not see that the spouses in a marriage are set in God's Word. They cannot see a wife and husband clothed in and outfitted with God's Word.

This is why marriage is not an honorable institution for

them. Rather, they attribute to marriage all that is shameful. For they are more pleased with a shameful fornicating way of life than with this divine and honorable way of life.

The apostle here warns Christians against this way of thinking so that among them marriage is kept gloriously and honorably as God's institution and ordinance. This is done by avoiding the life of fornication and entering the life of marriage.

They attribute to marriage all that is shameful

In marriage, it is done by keeping the marriage bed pure and undefiled. That happens when the wife stands by her husband and the husband is content with his wife. If this is not done, the beautiful adornment—that is, God's Word—is defiled by the devil's excrement and the marriage bed is stained as surely as if someone had actually defecated in it.

Therefore pay attention when the devil comes to you with carnal curiosity and gluttony. Be prudent and lay hold of God's Word. Think: God has created me as a man and placed me into marriage. This woman he has placed into my arms in order to be mine.

If you do this, you can easily keep your marriage bed pure. For the Word will make you fear and dislike, even abhor and loathe other women. This Word of God will also adorn your wife so that, even though she be terrible and hostile, impatient and hardheaded, she will be lovelier to you and please you more for the sake of the Word than another woman that is adorned with pure gold.

Therefore, the wedding dress is a precious dress, and a wedding tuxedo is a well-adorned suit for you if you can see it as such. This is what it means to honor and praise the institution of marriage rightly and to keep the marriage bed pure. For there is no honor or adornment or beauty or purity above God's Word.

---

1. What do those who live together think of marriage?
2. But in what are husband and wife truly outfitted?
3. How is the marriage bed kept pure and undefiled?
4. What will the Word of God make the Christian fear and dislike?
5. Why are the wedding dress and tuxedo precious and well-adorned?

9

So Why Even Get Married?

Nowadays there are many who are looking for excuses to avoid marriage and to drown finally in fornication. They claim that there are many bad things that happen in marriage, that there is much sinning in it in terms of anger, impatience, evil desires, etc.

No one denies this. No one says that marriage in its entirety occurs in purity, without any sin.

But according to this argument, I would have to stop preaching and workers would have to stop doing their jobs. And the government would have to stop using the sword.

But not so fast, my friend! In this life we will never be

so pure so as to do some work without any sin.

This article must stand firm: I believe in the forgiveness of sins. And daily we must say in the Lord's Prayer: Forgive us our trespasses.

Therefore, do not come up with excuses for avoiding this institution. Sin is sin. If you want to brand one institution as sinful, you should brand the other one likewise.

Yet if you want to make one exception, make an exception for the other as well. I never wish to have preached, or preach, a single sermon without sin. I will remain a sinner and wish to keep the article concerning the forgiveness of sins in place without denying it.

If spouses are at times angry with one another, it is indeed sin and injustice. Yet compared to this the forgiveness of sins is so much bigger—if they remain in marriage and do not leave it, living in the very institution into which God has called them. For even though marriage cannot take place without sin, God's Word is nonetheless so great that for its sake the institution is also pure and holy.

Compared to this the forgiveness of sins is so much bigger

Let me also say this: If you are getting at the fact that we are all born in sin from Adam, then the whole institution—even if it is kept rightly and well—is sinful and impure. It would be just as life is among the Pagans and the unbelievers who do not have the Word of God, where all life and work is sinful and condemnable before God.

Therefore, note well here that Paul speaks about this institution in this way—serving as the mouthpiece of

God—that it should be, and should be called, honorable and pure among the Christians, so long as fornication and adultery is avoided. For if one were to take Adam's fall and our nature into consideration, marriage would not be pure and honorable before God. For such carnal desire and other sinful inclination would not have existed in paradise.

Also, at that point no man would have disliked another or been ashamed before another. There also would not have been any need for coverings or adornments.

Rather, husband and wife would have stood by one another without any evil lust and desires. Easily and without effort and worries they would have begotten and born children, as one picks an apple from the tree.

No husband and wife come together without shameful lust

However, the way it is now is different: No husband and wife come together without shameful lust. This is why Ps. 51:5 says: "Behold, I was begotten from sinful seed, and my mother conceived me in sin." All the saints who have been married have had to confess that they were not exempt from such unwillingness.

Accordingly, Christ himself did not wish to be born in a natural way from a husband and wife. He therefore chose a virgin as his mother, sanctifying her flesh and blood so that his birth would be a pure, holy birth.

---

1. Why do people look for excuses to avoid marriage?
2. Does marriage occur without any sin?

3. Which article must stand firm?

4. Would there have been carnal desire and sinful inclination before the fall?

5. Can husband and wife come together without sin?

10

Marriage is Purified by God's Word

Yet now the apostle says here that God wishes to have the institution of marriage graced in such a way that it, although impure by nature, should nonetheless not be impure among those who are Christians and have faith. Rather, it should henceforth be called a pure marital bed.

Not on its own account or based on our nature. But God covers marriage with his grace and does not wish to impute the natural sin or impurity, which has been planted in us by the devil.

Therefore, God goes ahead and purifies marriage with his Word so that it now becomes a divine, holy institution.

He does not accomplish this by taking away lust or bridal love. Nor does God forbid marital relations (although these do not happen without sin) as the pope's teaching does.

The pope considered and taught that marriage was impure. Therefore no one was able to serve God while being married.

But God himself calls purified that which he declares pure out of grace and does not impute the sin that is in nature. It is just as he says to Peter in Acts 10:15: "Do not make impure what I have made pure." Here that which was otherwise impure and forbidden becomes pure and holy by virtue of God's speaking alone.

It is the same way in the case of marriage. Because God makes marriage pure by his speaking, calling it a chaste holy institution, we should also regard it as pure.

However, you need to know that such purity is not the result of nature. It is a result only of grace which covers and blots out the natural impurity and sin.

God does the same thing with all of original sin in those who are baptized and believe that they have the forgiveness of sins on account of the Savior Christ and become children of eternal life. For although this same original sin remains stuck in the flesh and remains active for as long as we live on earth, we who are Christians are called pure and holy because God makes the sign of the cross over us. Additionally he gives us his Holy Spirit who begins to drive out sin and who continues to do so until death.

God makes marriage pure by his speaking

Therefore, we are, to be sure, not without sin. Yet we

have the sentence from heaven, pronounced by God's mouth, that we now are pure and holy because we have been covered with, and enveloped in, the beautiful heaven of grace—that is, Christ with his purity, righteousness, and holiness spread over us—and have been incorporated into him by baptism and cling to him by faith.

God does the same thing, I say, in the case of the institution of marriage. Although sin and evil desires are present in it, even in the saints, God nevertheless covers the spouses with his cloak and pronounces them pure by his Word.

This is the beautiful cover that is spread over the marriage bed. It adorns it and on its account it is called a beautiful, pure, undefiled bed.

This is why the apostle admonishes those who live in this institution to think that, because God pronounces marriage to be pure and spreads such cover over it, they too should recognize this and be grateful for it. They also should see that they not make their marital bed—so purified, washed, and adorned by God—once again impure and defiled by adultery or fornication.

God nevertheless covers the spouses with his cloak

---

1. With what does God cover marriage?
2. How does God purify marriage?
3. Why should we regard marriage as pure and holy?

4. Why are we as Christians called pure and holy?

5. Are we then without sin?

11

So Marriage is to be Honored

Not only does God wish to have the marital bed declared to be pure. He also wishes marriage itself to be honored.

By so doing, God covers up the sinful desires and other shortcomings of marriage even more completely. So marriage is not only to be called pure, but it also, according to God's Word and command, is to be declared honorable and precious.

This is what it means to put bride and bridegroom to bed and cover them completely. This is what it means to adorn them most beautifully and to lead them to church most honorably. For here God clothes them in his adornment which is much more beautiful than all pieces of gold, pearls, and precious stones, namely, the Fourth Commandment. "You shall honor father and mother, etc." (Ex. 20:12), which also means to honor the institution of marriage.

God also dresses the bride and bridegroom in the Sixth Commandment, "You shall not commit adultery" (Ex. 20:14). By this commandment, God commands you to stand by your spouse and to be content with him or her. If you do that, God promises that marriage will not be called sin but a blessed institution that well pleases him.

Moreover, in Gen. 2 God confirms and binds marriage together so tightly that he even annuls—or at least attenuates—the justice and power of the parents by this institution. God does this when he says in verse 24: "This is why a man will leave father and mother and cling to his wife."

God commands you to stand by your spouse

Also, soon after the fall, God again blesses them, promising them the seed of the woman (cf. Gen. 3:15). And God clothes and adorns Adam and Eve himself (cf. Gen. 3:21).

And we see with our own eyes how God preserves as honorable this miserable flesh and blood. It is born and lives in sin, and yet God continually blesses it and makes it fertile.

So despite sin, all the saints come from the institution of marriage. In fact, this entire life springs from it.

This is also why to the first mother Eve was given that name which means "the living one" or "the mother of the living" (Gen. 3:20). And how could God praise marriage more highly than by calling it also pure and holy in the New Testament?

This is why we too should honor and glorify marriage. We certainly should not act like the impure swine which do not think or talk about marriage in any other way than about their shameful fornication and adultery. They are shameful, repulsive people who defecate in their own beds and who, like actual pigs, delight in going through excrement with their dirty snout and wallow in their own shame.

This is why we too should honor and glorify it

Christians, however, should keep this institution as honorable and beautiful as they see God himself do. If they find something in marriage that is impure, they should cover and adorn it, just as God himself does. They do so by not counting as sin that which is sinful and unclean by nature, but covering it with a blanket, making it beautiful and honorable.

In the same way, we also should not act like the hotheaded fools who with hostility reprove and criticize this beloved institution. They do so by noting that there is a lot of drudgery, conflict, labor, and effort in marriage. Such people cry out, "May God protect me from marriage! If you get married, you will live with a devil."

These are the ravenous dogs which rape marriage from the other side with their blasphemous mouths, just as those pigs defile it with their snouts. For the devil always finds what appears to be a good reason not to marry.

The devil, of course, recognizes in marriage 1) original

sin and 2) the misfortune, labor, and work that have been placed within it (cf. Gen. 3:16-19). He can take advantage of these two to cause all to despise the marital life and abandon it entirely.

This is why we must exalt the institution of marriage all the more. We must praise, adorn, and embellish it to the greatest extent, as we hear God himself do.

Let the devil go on and on and rape and blaspheme marriage by means of his pigs and dogs. Let them receive the wages that their god, the devil, will pay them.

Yet you should learn to view and hold marriage as it is purified and sanctified by God's Word, and as it is to be honored as God's work. And if you are married, take comfort in this fact and thank God that he is pleased to have it this way, namely, to cover it with the bedding or blanket and to adorn and praise it so gloriously and beautifully.

---

1. According to God's Word, what is marriage to be declared?
2. Which two commandments directly address marriage?
3. So despite sin, what springs from marriage?
4. Why should we honor and glorify marriage?
5. Who always finds what appears to be a good reason not to marry?
6. How is marriage purified and sanctified?

12

It is Like Christ's Spiritual Marriage to the Church

In Ephesians 5(:22-33) it says: *Let the wives be subject to their husband, as to the Lord. For the husband is the head of the wife, just as Christ is the head of the congregation. And he is the Savior of his body. Yet just as the congregation is subject to Christ, so also the wives should be to their husbands in all things.*

Husbands, love your wives, just as Christ has also loved the congregation and has given himself for it in order to sanctify it. And he has cleansed it by the water bath in the Word, in order to present it to himself a congregation that would be glorious, without spots or wrinkles or the like, but that it would be holy and faultless.

In the same way also the husbands should love their wives as their own bodies. He who loves his wife loves himself. For no one has ever hated his own flesh, but nourishes and takes care of it, just as the Lord does for the congregation.

For we are members of his body, of his flesh and of his bones. And "this is why a man will leave his father and mother and cling to his wife, and two will be one flesh." The mystery is great, but I speak of Christ and the congregation.

There are evil works that are not called evil

Yet you too, yes, let each love his wife as himself. But let the wife fear the husband.

Here St. Paul combines and weaves together these two topics: 1) Marriage and 2) The resurrection—along with the whole kingdom of Christ in his Christendom. And the Apostle places before those married, both husband and wife, this one example: Christ is the head of the church as a man is the head of his wife, and Christendom is his bride or wife.

In this way, Paul teaches us and all who would have Christian marriage and do a better job in it than the Pagans. We are to take a close look at this image which God has presented them in Christ and his Christendom.

We are to act accordingly in the institution of marriage, praising and thanking God that we are found actually to be in both divine institutions: We are in the exalted spiritual marriage with the Lord Christ. And we are in this lowly bodily marriage in the world or in the flesh.

Even though the Pagans praised and honored this institution over against fornication and adultery, they did not know anything about its exalted stature. They did not know that God holds marriage so highly. For God has woven himself into marriage by his own Son whereby he has united his Son with us.

God has woven himself into marriage by his own Son

This is why the Pagans were unable to consider marriage to be as honorable and glorious as do the Christians. Christians know that Christ himself is our bridegroom and that we—as members of Christendom, his bride—belong to this spiritual marriage.

This is also why this institution should be considered to be more honorable and glorious. Marriage is to be as highly praised, glorified, and exalted as this example of Christ and his Christendom.

So to honor Christ, we should guard all the more against fornication and other sins. We should keep marriage pure and holy, as St. Paul admonishes us in 1 Thess. 4:3-4: "This is God's will, your sanctification, that you avoid sexual immorality, and that each among you know how to keep his vessel in sanctification and honor."

He says, "Your sanctification." In other words: Keep yourself and your body holy. In it the soul is kept and lives as in a vessel.

Do not do as the Pagans. They do not know anything about God. They have a low view of this institution. And also do not do as many of those who are called Christians, but who in all things live like pigs and unreasonable beasts.

Rather, God says, honor your body and this bodily life both inside and outside of this institution. Consider the way God instituted marriage, according to the exalted, glorious image of Christ and Christendom, by which he has honored and sanctified it.

In this way you will behave accordingly and demonstrate your gratitude for enjoying marriage and participating in it.

After all, it is not an insignificant honor and glory for the institution of marriage when God presents it as the image and example of the exalted, unspeakable grace and love which he shows and gives us in Christ. God depicts marriage as the most certain and loveliest sign of the highest, friendliest union between him and Christendom which is closer than any other union.

God depicts marriage as the most certain and loveliest sign

God hereby demonstrates sufficiently that the institution of marriage is divinely established. It pleases him because he has chosen and established it to be just such a holy example or pattern of the spiritual marriage.

In marriage God's heart and will toward us is to shine forth. And we all are to see our reflection in this mirror daily. Spouses especially in their marital life should act accordingly, as St. Paul here admonishes them to do.

---

1. Which two topics does the Apostle Paul weave together in Ephesians 5?

2. With whom are we in a spiritual marriage?

3. Who is the bride of Christ?

4. Why are we to keep ourselves and our bodies holy?
5. Of what is marriage the most certain and loveliest sign?
6. How does God's heart and will shine forth to us in marriage?

13

As is the Christian Marriage

This is why St. Paul portrays marriage here with many beautiful and glorious words about the Christian marriage, as Christ has loved Christendom and prepared it to be his pure, beautiful bride, etc. As I said, Paul thus draws in Christ's resurrection by which he brought this about.

For Christ himself says to his apostles in John 20:21, 23: "As the Father has sent me, so I send you. If you forgive the sins of any, they are forgiven," etc. Here he himself establishes this spiritual marriage as a fruit and result of his resurrection.

This sending of the apostles, in plain English, means to

send out suitors who are to woo the bride and lead her to the bridegroom. Accordingly, Christ has chosen for himself a bride, St. Paul says here, the congregation or Christendom, and has prepared the same by the Word and water baptism.

Christ has chosen for himself a bride

This has been done by means of the apostles, sent out by Christ. The purpose of their office is to summon and call us to Christ. And also to cleanse and sanctify us in order to marry and unite us to him.

Along these lines, St. Paul boasts that he is just such a messenger or suitor. Paul is sent by Christ, as he says in 2 Cor. 11:2: "I am jealous for you with divine jealousy. For I have betrothed you to one man in order to present a pure virgin to Christ," etc.

By this, Paul himself shows that the office of an apostle is nothing but the office of a suitor or best man who daily prepares Christ's bride and leads her to him. This is like Abraham's servant who fetched a bride for Isaac, Gen. 24.

Such an office Christ first here, after his resurrection, entrusted to, and placed upon the apostles, as if he wanted to say thereby: I send you to summon and fetch a bride for me. But in a way that she might be prepared and washed before from sin, thus becoming pure and holy.

Now, this fetching, preparing and washing happens daily in Christendom by means of the preaching office. The preaching office proclaims and says, first, as St. Paul here says, that Christ has given himself for her.

This took place when Christ suffered and died on the cross and rose on the third day. For by doing so he earned for us grace and the forgiveness of sins.

Yet if Christ had left it at that, we still would not be helped. For although he had earned the treasure and done everything for us, we would still have not received it.

Yet how does it happen that the very sanctification which Christ accomplished comes to us? For he has now ascended to heaven and leaves us here below.

This is how it happens. Christ says: By the Word and baptism it must be brought home to us. This Christ commanded his apostles to bring to us, namely, that they should thereby bring to us the forgiveness of sins in his name.

In this way, Christ remains up on high at the right hand of the Father. But Christ still brings us to himself by his apostles and the preachers of the gospel, just as he brought to himself the congregation at Corinth, Ephesus, and many other places by means of St. Paul.

---

1. Of what is the Christian's spiritual wedding with Christ a fruit?

2. How were the apostles to act as suitors?

3. So how were the apostles like Abraham's servant?

4. How does this fetching, preparing and washing happen daily within Christendom?

5. How does the sanctification which Christ accomplished come to us?

14

Which the World Does Not Grasp

This is how the sanctification earned by Christ comes to us by means of the preaching office of the gospel and by means of baptism. And where the Word is preached and heard, there you hear the suitors of this bridegroom.

And if you accept and believe it, and are baptized upon it, you have already been brought to Christ as a bride. You have been prepared, cleansed, washed, and sanctified, as Christ wishes her to be.

Based on this command of Christ—that all those who believe the apostles' preaching concerning the forgiveness of sins are absolved and clean from sins—the entire world (as well as we ourselves) was brought to Christ and incorporated into Christendom, his bride. For even though we do not hear the apostles themselves, we do hear the selfsame Word of God and receive thereby the selfsame grace and sanctification.

For the Word of God as well as its effect and power do not belong to the apostles. It is instead Christ's own Word and work, as St. Paul also says here: "He (himself) has cleansed and sanctified it," not the apostle or other messengers and preachers.

It is instead Christ's own Word and work

The apostle and other messengers and preachers are much too lowly that they should wash and cleanse me. In fact, they themselves need such bathing and cleansing as much as I or anybody else.

Yet, says the apostle, we become pure and holy by means of this, that he, Christ, "has given himself for us" and has this now preached and offered to us by the Word. This is why it makes no difference to me by what kind of person—whether he is holy or not—and when and where Christ has this preached to me and has me baptized.

What is decisive alone is that it is the Word and baptism of the Lord Christ. Where this is preached to me, there I hear his servants who come to me on his behalf and bring me to him so that I become his bride.

This is now the great, unspeakable grace and gift, as St. Paul calls it here, which God has given to the Christians, even though it does not shine before the world. For you can figure out for yourself what an honor and glory it must be that Christ, God's Son, stoops so low and joins us in such a friendly way that he does not simply let himself be called our Lord, not even a father, brother, or friend.

This is now the great, unspeakable grace and gift

Instead, Christ, employing the name of the highest love and closest friendship on earth, wants to be, and be called, our bridegroom, and be with us one body—as one says about husband and wife—or, as Scripture puts it here, of one flesh and one bone. This is not said of any other relationship or friendship.

In this way, Christ wanted to show himself in the dearest and friendliest way toward us. He offers and promises his greatest love to us, so that we might be called his dear bride. And conversely, that we might call him our dear bridegroom and praise him with all confidence.

This is why St. Paul gives such a glorious sermon about this spiritual marriage. He magnifies it so much, as if it could not sufficiently be expressed by words, concluding it by saying: "This mystery is great."

He means to say here that it is an exceedingly lofty, glorious, unspeakable thing that God signifies by marriage. "Yet I say," he says, "in Christ and Christendom," that is, in this spiritual marriage.

"Mystery," however, means a hidden, secret thing, which is known only in the spirit. So it is known only by faith and according to the Word of God. Not by reason or according to the appearance.

For no one can presently see or feel what kind of a queen I have become, if I believe in Christ, by means of the Word and baptism. Why? These two things appear to be so utterly humble and simple.

In short, the marriage as well as the bride and bridegroom, along with all the treasures and goods which are received in this spiritual marriage, are secret and hidden from us. It is too lofty and far from human reason and senses that here such great, glorious things should be accomplished.

These two things appear to be so utterly humble and simple

In brief, this spiritual marriage cannot be known or grasped except by two external items: The Word of God and water. For, to be sure, I hear this sermon, how God has thus graced me by Christ as his bride, giving me a share in all his heavenly and eternal goods. I also see that you are baptized on this basis.

Yet when I look at you, I do not see anything of this sort. For here I see nothing except that you live a life in the body, that you eat and drink, work, and do everything in this external life like any other human being.

In all this you are just like a Pagan. So I cannot see the glory and adornment with which Christ has clothed you.

You too cannot see more of them than what you grasp by faith. And if we could see and experience what we have here, I think we would already be in heaven.

For what greater joy and blessedness could there be for a human being than to be able to rely with certainty and without doubt, and to boast wholeheartedly, that Christ is one body with me and shares everything he has and can with me, as a bridegroom does with his wife. There everything is in common and undivided: Body, possessions and honor.

All other friends and social institutions break up and go their own ways. Children leave their parents. Brothers and sisters leave from one house and inheritance.

Yet marriage binds and keeps everything together. For the sake of marriage you leave father and mother and everything else. In marriage, one joins the other also with one's own life, if it is true marital love.

Yet marriage binds and keeps everything together

This is what Christ did for his congregation, says St. Paul. He loved it and gave himself for it so that we might be one body with him and have everything in him. And so that we might appropriate Christ for ourselves and find comfort in him and all his heavenly glory as our own.

---

1. Does the Word of God with its effects and powers belong to the apostles?

2. By what means do we become pure and holy?

3. Does the unspeakable gift given to Christians by God shine before the world?

4. What does *mystery* mean?

5. How can the spiritual marriage of the Christian with Christ be known and grasped?

6. What did Christ do for his congregation?

15

The Christian's Spiritual Marriage is Glorious

Oh this spiritual marriage is a great and glorious thing. Who can sufficiently express and grasp it? Who can consider that an old bag of maggots, conceived and born in sin, should receive such glory? That it should be called a bride of the majesty in heaven, namely, God's Son, who has united himself with us in such a way that everything he is and has is ours? Meanwhile, everything we are and have also becomes his.

Yet what is he? Or what are we?

He is the handsome bridegroom, utterly pure without any defect. He is the Lord over all creatures, eternal righteousness, eternal power, and eternal life.

In summary, he is an utterly eternal incomprehensible good which no heart can ever sufficiently grasp and consider. Both angels and men have something to see in him into all eternity.

He is an utterly eternal incomprehensible good

By comparison, we are poor miserable creatures filled with sin and filth. We are corrupted from head to toe, through and through. We are subject to the devil and condemned to death and damnation under God's wrath.

This is why it must surely be an unspeakable grace. In fact, it must be the pure fire and desire of love which cause God to stoop so low and to give himself to us willingly and to make it so costly for himself to bring us to himself. He is not afraid to shed his precious blood and to suffer the most shameful death so that we might be called his bride and possess his goods.

What are those goods? They are: Eternal righteousness, freedom, blessedness and life instead of sin, death, and the power of the devil in which we lay.

Here Christ clothes us in all his purity in order to set us free from sin. He clothes us in all his honor in order to cover and take away our shame. He clothes us in his body and life in order to rescue us from death. He clothes us in all his heavenly possessions and power in order to bring us from this needy, miserable life to his glory.

This also means that the sin and shortcomings, which still are in us, shall not harm us. The devil shall not accuse us. The law shall not damn us. Death shall not kill us.

For Christ stands in front of us, saying: "Leave my bride in peace. If there is any shortcoming in her, I will make up for it. If she is not beautiful and pure enough, I will make her beautiful and pure.

It doesn't matter if you do not like her. It is enough that I do.

For I have chosen and cleansed her for myself. I continually cleanse her daily by the Word and baptism.

If she still has sin, death, and other shortcomings in herself, I have the remedy of righteousness, life, and all eternal possessions. With them I adorn her so that she may possess them as her own."

See, these are the high, heavenly treasures and possessions that are praised here. Yet they are and remain what St. Paul calls a mystery, or a hidden, secret good which the world neither sees nor knows.

It is so great that even the Christians, who grasp it by the Word in faith, cannot reach or comprehend it. If you could fully grasp it in your heart, you would not be able to live long on earth for joy.

Yet there is the wretched misery in our flesh and blood. It does not let us get into these glorious thoughts so that we could rightly contemplate it and consider it to be as great as it is in itself.

Our heart is much too narrow and too weak. And the glory of the spiritual marriage is much too great to be comprehended by us.

Our heart is much too narrow and too weak

Just so the bridegroom Christ, and his purity and glory which he has, is much too great. And the love for us which he demonstrates in this is incomprehensible.

Still, we derive from it this great comfort that Christ also bears our daily weakness and lets us be excused by it, so long as we cling to him. For he still must daily and always cleanse us.

And wherever there are still wrinkles and blemishes, Christ applies the salve of his righteousness and purity that we might still retain the glory, being gladly able to confess him as our bridegroom and say: "No matter what my condition might be, I will remain where my dear bridegroom remains.

If anybody finds a fault in me, let him talk to Christ. For Christ wishes, and lets me be told, that I will remain his bride if I believe in him. Christ has brought me to this point by the Word and baptism, which he has given me through my dear preachers."

This is and shall be the Christians' sermon to praise, honor, and thank God that he shows himself so graciously toward us. And has given himself to us.

For, as has been said sufficiently, in this spiritual marriage is contained everything he has and is able to give. By it, Christ has made it a common good and joint possession among him and us.

All Christ's righteousness becomes ours

All Christ's righteousness becomes ours. All our sin and shortcomings become his, as he has richly demonstrated and still demonstrates.

For in Christ, God has taken upon himself and carried

the sin of the entire world, mine and yours included. As St. Paul says in 2 Cor. 5:21, "him who knew of no sin he made himself sin so that we would in him become the righteousness that avails before God." He has sent out his preachers to bring this home to us by the Word and baptism.

---

1. What is the result of our spiritual union with the Son of God?
2. What are we in comparison to the incomprehensible good of the Son of God?
3. What are the goods that the Son of God would share with us?
4. Is the love that Christ the bridegroom expresses for us comprehensible?
5. What has God done for us in Christ?

16

For the Church is the Bride of Christ

Therefore, let us learn to boast in this marriage as Christians. We are to know its treasure and glory. Let us take comfort in it. Let us rejoice that by God's grace we have come to the great honors of being, and being called, the bride of his Son Christ.

I conclude this from the fact that I have the Word and baptism and have begun to believe. And if I stick to it, I am certain that God has adopted me for this, has adorned me with his adornment, has taken away all wrinkles and blemishes, and still always cleanses me more and more.

Now that you have become his bride, you have the keys

and are the lady of the house and sit among his heavenly possessions. It is as St. Paul says in Eph. 1:18, so that neither sin nor death nor devil have furthermore any claim or power over you (cf. Eph. 1:20-23).

You have the keys and are the lady of the house

See, such an exalted sermon and precious example St. Paul teaches us to discuss and expound upon the institution of marriage. According to that example, we should instruct those who are about to enter into marriage.

We should also remind those who are already married, concerning these things, so that they, when they look at their marriage, might think of these words and place this image or example of the spiritual marriage before their own eyes. For this might well be called a great, glorious marriage and a precious, noble adornment. Yet the way is secret and hidden, by which is brought to us, not bodily possessions, but the redemption from sin and death, and the communion of all divine possessions.

By comparison, however, all bodily adornment and treasures of this world are much too insignificant, even if you had many tons of gold, even the treasures of all the emperors and kings. For you can still grasp their ultimate value.

Moreover, the bodily bride and bridegroom are also not so precious. For they are poor mortal beings.

Still, such external, visible forms of the bodily marriage should serve the purpose of helping you to learn to contemplate and consider the spiritual marriage. That marriage's glory and adornment no one can completely grasp.

And, conversely, we should see our reflection in the spiritual union between Christ and Christendom. We thereby learn how spouses should behave towards one another in their marriage.

Marriage's glory and adornment no one can completely grasp

This is why St. Paul now gives to the spouses also their text, saying: Just as the congregation is subject to the Lord, so the wives should also be subject to their husbands. Also, "husbands, love your wives as Christ has loved the congregation."

This is to say that both parties should look how both Christ and his Christendom behave toward one another. For this is the highest and most perfect example and a true, clear mirror.

And then let them follow this example in all diligence. For there you see that Christ loves his congregation so that he also gives himself for it.

We will not even come close to this love. For, as has been said, it is much too exalted and great.

And just as the bodily marriage is small, so also the love in it is small when compared to Christ's. It must be enough to just follow this example according to the measure of this marriage, so that everybody in the institution of marriage has set his mind on showing and practicing love toward his bride or spouse.

And if there is some shortcoming or fault in her, let him excuse it and handle it reasonably, thinking: What should I do to her? She is my bride. I too must cover, cleanse, adorn, and improve here as much as I can and show the little love in this small marriage, just as Christ shows the high, unspeakable love toward his bride of whom I am a member as well.

Again, St. Paul says, the wife should be subject and obedient to the husband "just as the congregation is to Christ." There he does not command the bride or the wife to love, but to honor her husband and to be subject to him, which evidently cannot be done without love.

For I deny honor and every good thing to the person I do not love. I will also not show him much obedience or service.

Therefore, if it is to be true honor and submission it must flow from love that the wife might know and be convinced that the husband is higher and better than her. For the rule and the upper hand belong to the husband as the head and the master of the household, as St. Paul says elsewhere: "The husband is God's honor and God's image" (1 Cor. 11:7). And in 1 Cor. 11:9 he says: "The husband was not created for the wife but the wife for the husband."

This is why there should be this difference: The husband should certainly love the wife, but not be subject to her. The wife, however, should also honor and fear the husband, in all discipline and respect.

For this is also how Christendom behaves in that it holds the bridegroom Christ in all honor as its Lord and head. And it obeys Christ and submits to him in all things.

This is also how Christendom behaves

In other words, it remains in the pure faith, lives according to Christ's commandment, and does everything it knows he wants done. That is, unless the devil enters in and changes the bride's mind, as St. Paul is concerned about his church, saying in 2 Cor. 11:2-3: "'I have made you a true bride and presented you to Christ,' but there is something that bothers me and I am concerned about you.

In fact, I am so envious and jealous about you—but with a divine jealousy, not out of anger or hatred—that I begrudge you everybody else. For I fear nothing more than that the devil woo you and tear you away from Christ, just as happened to Eve in paradise.

She also was a beautiful bride, adorned with all sorts of things, both external and spiritual, divine adornments, also being obedient and subject to God. Yet the devil seduced her and caused her to fall so that she fell away from God and followed the adulterer, leading all of us with her into the predicament in which we now find ourselves.

This is how I am concerned about you," Paul says, "who have now been brought back to Christ and have become his bride." The danger is great because the devil assaults Christendom without ceasing and because we are weak. Therefore, you must diligently be on guard and see to it that you do not let yourselves be led away by Satan's deceit and cunning from the Word and obedience of your dear Lord Christ, who has loved you and given himself for you.

Do not let yourselves be led away by Satan's deceit

---

1. In that Christians have become the bride of Christ, what do they possess?

2. Should those who are to be married be instructed in the spiritual marriage to Christ?
3. For what purpose do the visible forms of bodily marriage serve?
4. In order to honor someone, must we love them?
5. How does Christendom behave in view of Christ?

17

The Christian's Spiritual Marriage Shapes Marriage

We see how nowadays and always Christians are seduced by many a sectarian group. We also see how up to this time the entire world was totally filled with institutes of spiritual fornication and adultery under the papacy.

Christ's bride had been corrupted to the point of being unrecognizable. Now Christ has once again begun to cleanse her by his Word.

Christ has once again begun to cleanse her by his Word

See, this is what it means for Christendom to be obedient and subject to Christ in all things: So that it might closely stand by him alone and follow only his Word. And not follow those who wish to teach and lead it differently.

Accordingly also in the institution of marriage, the wife should not only love the husband but also obey him and submit to him so as to let herself be governed and bow before him. In short, she is to stand by him and follow him, not looking only to the husband's authority, as her head, but also place before herself this example.

The example of the Christian's spiritual marriage to Christ should remind her to think like this: "My husband is an image of the true, high head Christ. For the sake of the latter I will honor the former and do what pleases him."

In the same way also, the husband should love his wife wholeheartedly for the sake of the great love which he sees here in Christ who has given himself for us. The husband should also think: "Neither I nor anyone else has ever done something like this. I will therefore do as much as I can according to the example. I will behave toward my wife in a loving manner as toward my own flesh in order to care for her, feed her, and provide for her.

It is a picture of the great spiritual marriage of Christ

I will not act bitterly or strangely toward her but, although she might be with frailties and faults, bear with her in a reasonable and patient manner or make her better by friendly admonitions and rebukes."

Where this happens, it would then no longer be a worldly and human or reasonable marriage but a Christian, divine marriage about which the Pagans know nothing. For they do not see the precious adornment and great honor of the marriage, namely, that it is a picture of the great spiritual marriage of Christ.

Therefore, as I said, it behooves us as Christians to honor and glorify this institution much more because we are the ones who know the great adornment and glory which are attached to it.

Do not be surprised when the world, as it wallows in fornication and adultery, and also the false, mad saints, consider marriage to be insignificant.

Yet we should justly consider marriage to be the greatest of all institutions of human life. For no other such institution has been utilized by God for such an exalted image.

We know that those who despise marriage, especially when they wish to be called Christians, not only create shame before the world but also bring dishonor and shame upon the exalted holy marriage between Christ and Christendom. They show in sufficient clarity that they think very little of the latter because they despise the former, humble as it is.

Let this be enough for this time on this text of St. Paul where he admonishes the Christians to consider this and to look at their marriage not only according to its external forms, as the world and carnal hearts do. But Christians are to contemplate in marriage something that is larger and greater, namely, the beautiful comforting image of Christ and Christendom.

Christians are to do this so that they might keep this institution of marriage as something precious and honorable—not only because God has ordained and commanded it thus, but also to honor the great spiritual marriage, so as

For we are not to let such glory and comfort be taken out of our sight

to demonstrate that they would like to be found in the latter. For we are not to let such glory and comfort be taken out of our sight and hearts, or cast it into a corner, as did the monks and the nuns, who applied marriage only to themselves.

They established their false, self-made spirituality instead, pretending that they alone were the brides of Christ, to despise and diminish the institution of marriage. Contrariwise, St. Paul does the opposite preaching such a great example to those united in marriage.

---

1. How does Christ cleanse his bride, the church?
2. Whose image is that of the husband in Christian marriage?
3. Whose image is that of the wife?
4. What does the world think of marriage?
5. What larger and greater thing is the Christian to contemplate in marriage?

Afterword

Marriage as Institution

For the Reformer of the Christian church, Martin Luther (1483-1546), marriage was more than a private arrangement between two consenting adults. Marriage was consensual, to be sure. Yet by a public vow two adults (male and female) entered what to this day is called a peculiar *Stand* in German. *Stand* is related to the Latin *status*, which is also common in English, denoting the social, legal, or civil status, that is, the place or position of a person within the whole of the social order. In other words, it refers to a social structure, order, or institution. This order exists as something one enters as a preexistent and common entity because it has been instituted or established and preserved by God. It entails duties and rights—a certain way of living one's life in accordance with one's status. Consequently, marriage is commonly subsumed under the broader category of "marital status." One also speaks of the "institution" of marriage, not as a social tradition but as an objective social reality.

This fundamental understanding of marriage as a God-given, common institution within mankind precludes viewing marriage and the married life as something subject to constant reinvention or redesign by each newly married couple, each new generation, or simply by chance social developments in the (evolutionary) course of human history. This basic notion also allows Luther to draw a clear distinction between marriage and cohabitation: While the public appearance and manner of life might be deceptively similar, the underlying difference in status makes all the difference; while the institution of marriage is ordained by God, cohabitation is not. And while the married way of life is appropriate for those who have publicly entered into the institution of marriage, it is ultimately deadly for those who have not.

In this way, understanding marriage as a divinely established special status or institution in society corresponds to how Luther views the whole of human life as lived in certain pre-established vocations (*Berufe*) and duties or offices (*Ämter*):[1] Each comes with its set of obligations and rights which are normally off limits for those persons not holding a particular vocation or office. In the text at hand, e.g., Luther illustrates the difference between marriage and cohabitation by pointing to the difference between a judge and a murderer: Both are able to take a human life, but only the former does so in a way that pleases God because only he has the divinely established vocation, office, and duty to do what he as a private person must never do. His particular status or place in society as a government official, one could say, gives him the right and duty to take the life of the guilty in capital cases—a duty and power he does not have as a private citizen.

In general, then, Christian ethics is not only about doing some abstract "right thing." It is also about doing the right thing at the concrete "right place in life" where a Christian might find himself. In the *Small Catechism*'s section on confession and absolution, Luther expresses this as follows: "Consider your place in life according to the Ten Commandments: Are you a father, mother, son, daughter, husband, wife, or worker?" These are concrete examples of the "holy orders and positions," as they are called in the heading of the Table of Duties section of the *Small Catechism*. In that section, Luther, simply by quoting key biblical verses, demonstrates that they all have their specific

[1] The German word *Amt* has a basic meaning similar to the Latin *officium*, namely, service or duty. Formal English usage still preserves this meaning, e.g., when speaking of the "offices" by which one obtained something.

duties, according to God's Word.

Based on Rom. 13:9, these duties, while they often seem contradictory (only compare the vocations of nurse and soldier), are consonant with, and summarized as, love. This "common order of Christian love," as Luther called it elsewhere, embraces the three basic holy orders of domestic life, civil life, and ecclesiastical life as well as everything not covered by them, such as helping every needy person in general. Christian love is the sphere of sanctification, not justification.[2]

Defining Marriage

Since confusion regarding the nature and purpose of marriage exists today, it is perhaps best to offer a brief definition of marriage that is gleaned from the numerous pertinent writings of Luther. It turns out that what marriage is all about was also unclear at Luther's time. Accordingly, he had to be clear in his teaching and could not assume some "traditional" consensus on what this divine institution is about.

For Luther, then, marriage is a public status ordained by God in paradise; it is therefore entered publicly.[3] It is a life-long covenant of fidelity,[4] entered freely by a consenting man and a con-

---

[2] Cf. AE 37:364-365.

[3] Cf. AE 46:283-284: "Because marriage is a public estate ordained by God and not a shady business to be carried on in dark corners, he who seeks it in corners and dark places or enters into it secretly is a marriage-thief, for he has stolen it and not obtained it honestly from God and through obedience to his word, as is fitting so honorable an estate. Therefore a marriage obtained by treachery and stealth, secretly and dishonestly, should yield to one obtained openly and honestly with God and honor. This is what must and shall be our rule in this matter, that private arrangements must yield to public ones, other things being equal; that is to say, secret betrothals shall yield to public ones. Likewise, living together in secret shall yield to that which is public."

[4] Cf. AE 44:10-11: "The whole basis and essence of marriage is that each gives himself or herself to the other, and they promise to remain faithful to

senting woman,[5] usually not against but with parental consent.[6] It is instituted chiefly for begetting children and raising them to fear and glorify the one true God.[7] However, after the fall, it also

---

each other and not give themselves to any other. By binding themselves to each other, and surrendering themselves to each other, the way is barred to the body of anyone else, and they content themselves in the marriage bed with their one companion."

[5] Cf. AE 44:11: "[T]he estate of marriage consists essentially in consent having been freely and previously given one to another." Also cf. AE 45:386: "To hinder or prevent a marriage is something quite different from compelling or forcing a marriage. Even if parents had the right and authority to do the first, that is, to prevent a marriage, it does not follow that they also have the authority to compel a marriage. It is more tolerable that the love which two have for one another be hindered and broken up, than that two be forced together who have no love for one another. In the first instance the grief is but temporary. It is to be feared that the second, however, involves an eternal hell and a lifetime of misery."

[6] Cf. AE 45:392: "Where [marriage matters] proceed in Christian fashion there will be knowledge and consent on both sides: the father will not bestow his child without the child's knowledge and consent (as it is written in Genesis 24[:57–58], where Rebekah was asked beforehand and freely consented to become the wife of Isaac); the child in turn will not bestow himself without the father's knowledge and consent."

[7] Cf. AE 44:12: "[M]arriage produces offspring, for that is the end and chief purpose of marriage." See also AE 45:46: "… the greatest good in married life, that which makes all suffering and labor worthwhile, is that God grants offspring and commands that they be brought up to worship and serve him. In all the world this is the noblest and most precious work, because to God there can be nothing dearer than the salvation of souls. Now since we are all duty bound to suffer death, if need be, that we might bring a single soul to God, you can see how rich the estate of marriage is in good works. God has entrusted to its bosom souls begotten of its own body, on whom it can lavish all manner of Christian works. Most certainly father and mother are apostles, bishops, and priests to their children, for it is they who make them acquainted with the gospel. In short, there is no greater or nobler authority on earth than that of parents over their children, for this authority is both spiritual and temporal. Whoever teaches the gospel to another is truly his apostle and bishop. Mitre and staff and great estates indeed produce idols,

serves as a remedy against sinful lust.[8] While Christians have learned to regard it as a figure of Christ's union with his bride, the Church,[9] and while it is divine as to its institution, it is in itself a worldly, bodily estate pertaining to the First Article of the Creed,[10] for which the secular government, not the church,

---

but teaching the gospel produces apostles and bishops. See therefore how good and great is God's work and ordinance!" Furthermore cf. AE 1:115-116, 118: "But here there is a question: 'When God says: »It is not good that man should be alone,« of what good could He be speaking, since Adam was righteous and had no need of a woman as we have, whose flesh is leprous through sin?' My answer is that God is speaking of the common good or that of the species, not of personal good. The personal good is the fact that Adam had innocence. But he was not yet in possession of the common good which the rest of the living beings who propagated their kind through procreation had. For so far Adam was alone; he still had no partner for that magnificent work of begetting and preserving his kind. ... So the woman was a helper for Adam; for he was unable to procreate alone, just as the woman was also unable to procreate alone. Moreover, these are the highest praises of sex, that the male is the father in procreation, but the woman is the mother in procreation and the helper of her husband."

[8] Cf. AE 28:10-11: "Although it is true that there is attraction and temptation wherever men and women are together, the matter is not helped by separating them. For how does it help me if I do not see, hear, or touch a woman and still my heart is full of women and my thoughts are taken up with them day and night, thinking of the shameless things that one might do? And of what help is it to a girl to shut her up so that she neither sees nor hears a man, when her heart still sighs day and night, without ceasing, for a young man? One has to have the heart for chastity, otherwise all such things are worse than hell and purgatory. ... this suffering is a sinful suffering that one cannot bear in good conscience, for in itself it is sin and wrong. Therefore there is no help or counsel for it except to escape it and get rid of it. This can be achieved through marriage and in no other way."

[9] Cf. AE 36:95: "Christ and the church are, therefore, a mystery, that is, a great and secret thing which can and ought to be represented in terms of marriage as a kind of outward allegory. But marriage ought not for that reason to be called a sacrament."

[10] Cf. AE 53:112: "Since hitherto it has been customary to surround the consecration of monks and nuns with such great ceremonial display (even

ought to provide specific regulations within the parameters of this general definition.[11]

Challenges to Marriage

As today, marriage in Luther's day was not only a confused matter. It was also not without challenges. *There was, first of all, fornication.* If practiced within the context of cohabitation, it not only looked like the real McCoy, it was also given a scientific-sounding rationale that might still appeal to people today. It had reached such levels that Luther, in his 1535-1545 *Lectures on Genesis*, felt compelled to liken the situation in 16th-century Germany to what went on in OT Sodom (AE 3:254):

> [Lot] alone feared God, and in his house he maintained discipline and chastity to the utmost of his ability, while the others indulged freely and without shame in adultery, fornication, effeminacy, and even incest to such an extent that these were not regarded as sins but as some pastime, just as today among the nobility and the lower classes of Germany fornication is regarded as a pastime, not as a sin, and for this reason is also entirely unpunished.
>
> First in Italy and then by some canons in Germany it was argued that simple fornication of an unattached man with an unattached woman is not a sin but is a cleansing of nature, which seeks an outlet. Let this be said with due respect for

---

though their estate and organization are an ungodly and purely human invention which does not have any foundation in the Scriptures), how much more should we honor this divine estate and gloriously bless and embellish it and pray for it. For though it is a worldly estate, yet does it have God's word in its favor and was not invented or instituted by men, as was the estate of the monks and nuns."

[11] Cf. AE 46:265: "No one can deny that marriage is an external, worldly matter, like clothing and food, house and property, subject to temporal authority, as the many imperial laws enacted on the subject prove."

innocent ears, for I do not relish dealing with these matters. Yet we must be on our guard lest such shocking utterances carry away and ruin the age that is rash and in general is inclined toward sin. For where people live and teach in such a way and vices become customary, there, says Seneca sternly, there is no room for a cure.

Earlier in his *Lectures on Genesis*, Luther traced this careless attitude toward the actual sin of fornication to carelessness toward original sin, which is less fearsome and formidable if it is, like in Roman Catholic theology, declared to be something that does not destroy man's natural abilities because its opposite, original righteousness, is not viewed as an original part of human nature but as some superadded gift of grace. According to Luther, not only can sinful man not get rid of this natural sin, he also cannot even recognize it properly in all its deep-seated ramifications.[12] This leads sinful man to declare sinning—e.g., fornication—to be something beneficial for man. Luther stated (AE 1:166-167):

> But see what follows if you maintain that original righteousness was not a part of nature but a sort of superfluous or superadded gift. When you declare that righteousness was not a part of the essence of man, does it not also follow that sin, which took its place, is not part of the essence of man either? Then there was no purpose in sending Christ, the Redeemer, if the original righteousness, like something foreign to our nature, has been taken away and the natural endowments remain perfect. What can be said that is more unworthy of a theologian?
>
> Therefore let us shun those ravings like real pests and a

[12] Cf. SA III, II, 4: "… the chief function or power of the law is to make original sin manifest and show man to what utter depths his nature has fallen and how corrupt it has become. So the law must tell him that he neither has nor cares for God or that he worships strange gods — something that he would not have believed before without a knowledge of the law."

> perversion of the Holy Scriptures, and let us rather follow experience, which shows that we are born from unclean seed and that from the very nature of the seed we acquire ignorance of God, smugness, unbelief, hatred against God, disobedience, impatience, and similar grave faults. These are so deeply implanted in our flesh, and this poison has been so widely spread through flesh, body, mind, muscles, and blood, through the bones and the very marrow, in the will, in the intellect, and in reason, that they not only cannot be fully removed but are not even recognized as sin.
>
> There is a familiar saying of the comic poet: "No infamy attaches to a young man if he commits fornication." The pagan must be forgiven, but it is most shameful for Christians and those who are familiar with the Holy Scriptures to incline to the opinion that simple fornication is not a sin. The colleges of the canons unanimously approve this same opinion by their life and habits! When this happens in the case of an outward sin, what conclusion shall we reach about the uncleanness of the heart and the inner emotions which ungodly men do not realize to be sins?
>
> Similarly, man does not realize that the glory of nakedness was lost through sin. The fact that Adam and Eve walked about naked was their greatest adornment before God and all the creatures. Now, after sin, we not only shun the glance of men when we are naked; but we are also bashful in our own presence, just as Moses states here about Adam and Eve. This shame is a witness that our heart has lost the trust in God which they who were naked had before sin. Therefore even if Adam had been blind, he still would have been afraid to show himself naked to the eyes of God and of men, because through his disobedience his confidence in God was lost.

Evidently, for Luther, "simple fornication"—sexual intercourse among two "unattached" partners that therefore, strictly speaking, did not involve the still-acknowledged sin of adultery—is sin, based on biblical texts such as 1 Cor. 6:9 and Hebr. 13:4.[13] Luther's follow-up observation that sinful "man does not realize that the glory of nakedness was lost through sin" was no doubt evidenced for him by Renaissance's rediscovery of Antiquity's praise of the naked man. In a thoroughly sexualized society such as ours this observation becomes once again evident and equally difficult to correct (AE 3:254): "For where people live and teach in such a way and vices become customary, there, says Seneca sternly, there is no room for a cure."

There was, second, adultery. If fornication is defined as a sin only if it breaks an existing marriage (*Ehebruch*, adultery), then the situation is similar to what Christ encountered in his days on earth: Vices are sins only in their narrowest definition. Luther noted that Christ spoke out against this all-too-human way of eliminating sin in the Sermon of the Mount, where he teaches that even the lustful gaze at a woman other than one's own wife is already adultery. The remedy against this lust is not self-chosen isolation or ineffective vows of celibacy but the art of marriage, that is, the kind of marriage where the spouses regard one another, most beautifully adorned by God's Word itself, "as a divine gift and treasure" (AE 21:87). In the sermons translated in this booklet, Luther will expound on the art of marriage in greater detail.

There was, third, a reluctance to beget children, which Luther detected especially among the nobility, the wealthy and powerful of his day (AE 1:118):

> Today you find many people who do not want to have children. Moreover, this callousness and inhuman attitude, which is worse than barbarous, is met with chiefly among the nobility and princes, who often refrain from marriage for

[13] Cf. WA TR 2:162-163, recounting the query of a Bohemian guest at Luther's table concerning this very matter.

this one single reason, that they might have no offspring. It is even more disgraceful that you find princes who allow themselves to be forced not to marry, for fear that the members of their house would increase beyond a definite limit. Surely such men deserve that their memory be blotted out from the land of the living. Who is there who would not detest these swinish monsters? But these facts, too, serve to emphasize original sin. Otherwise we would marvel at procreation as the greatest work of God, and as a most outstanding gift we would honor it with the praises it deserves.

What seems to be a mere command—"be fruitful and multiply" (Gen. 1:28)—is thus more than that: It is God's work and ordinance, implanted in the very way man and woman have been created by God. One cannot voluntarily opt out of this creaturely reality and necessity. If this is attempted, without God's gracious gift of continence, based on human decisions, pledges, and vows[14] (no matter how well-intentioned), more sin is sure to follow (AE 45:18):

> ...this word which God speaks, "Be fruitful and multiply," is not a command. It is more than a command, namely, a divine ordinance [werck] which it is not our prerogative to hinder or ignore. Rather, it is just as necessary as the fact that I am a man, and more necessary than sleeping and waking, eating and drinking, and emptying the bowels and bladder. It is a nature and disposition just as innate as the organs involved

[14] Cf. AE 45:19: "Don't let yourself be fooled on this score, even if you should make ten oaths, vows, covenants, and adamantine or ironclad pledges. For as you cannot solemnly promise that you will not be a man or a woman (and if you should make such a promise it would be foolishness and of no avail since you cannot make yourself something other than what you are), so you cannot promise that you will not produce seed or multiply, ... And should you make such a promise, it too would be foolishness and of no avail, for to produce seed and to multiply is a matter of God's ordinance [*geschöpffe*], not your power."

in it. Therefore, just as God does not command anyone to be a man or a woman but creates them the way they have to be, so he does not command them to multiply but creates them so that they have to multiply. And wherever men try to resist this, it remains irresistible nonetheless and goes its way through fornication, adultery, and secret sins, for this is a matter of nature and not of choice.

Despising God's "greatest work" of procreation and the children resulting from it led, *fourth, to a generally inimical relation between the sexes and a negative attitude toward marriage.*[15] Women, and wives, were often exposed to scorn and ridicule. This inheritance of classical antiquity[16] centuries of Christianity had not erased (AE 45:36-37):

> There are many pagan books which treat of nothing but the depravity of womankind and the unhappiness of the estate of marriage, such that some have thought that even if Wisdom itself were a woman one should not marry. A Roman official was once supposed to encourage young men to take wives (because the country was in need of a large population on account of its incessant wars). Among other things he said to them, "My dear young men, if we could only live without women we would be spared a great deal of annoyance; but since we cannot do without them, take to yourselves wives," etc. ... So they concluded that woman is a necessary evil, and that no household can be without such an evil. These are the words of blind heathen, who are ignorant of the fact that man and woman are God's creation. ... I imagine that if women were to write books they would say exactly the

[15] Cf. AE 1:118: "[The desire to be childless] is also the source of the aspersions against the female sex, aspersions which ungodly celibacy has augmented."

[16] Cf. AE 1:70: "This ... fits Aristotle's designation of woman as a 'maimed man'; others declare that she is a monster."

same thing about men. What they have failed to set down in writing, however, they express with their grumbling and complaining whenever they get together.

> Every day one encounters parents who forget their former misery because, like the mouse, they have now had their fill. They deter their children from marriage but entice them into priesthood and nunnery, citing the trials and troubles of married life. Thus do they bring their own children home to the devil, as we daily observe; they provide them with ease for the body and hell for the soul.

These pagan notions continued to enjoy popularity in Luther's day because that which made, and makes, them popular is a constant factor in humans after the fall: depraved reason. Wrote Luther (AE 45:39):

> We err in that we judge the work of God according to our own feelings, and regard not his will but our own desire. This is why we are unable to recognize his works and persist in making evil that which is good, and regarding as bitter that which is pleasant. Nothing is so bad, not even death itself, but what it becomes sweet and tolerable if only I know and am certain that it is pleasing to God.[17] Then there follows immediately that of which Solomon speaks, "He obtains favor from the Lord" [Prov. 18:22].
>
> Now observe that when that clever harlot, our natural reason (which the pagans followed in trying to be most clever), takes a look at married life, she turns up her nose and says, "Alas, must I rock the baby, wash its diapers, make its bed, smell its stench, stay up nights with it, take care of it when it cries, heal its rashes and sores, and on top of that care for my wife, provide for her, labor at my trade, take care

[17] A better translation of this sentence is (cf. WA 10.2:295): "Nothing is so evil, even death itself, that it does not become sweet and bearable if I only know and am certain that it is pleasing to God."

> of this and take care of that, do this and do that, endure this and endure that, and whatever else of bitterness and drudgery married life involves? What, should I make such a prisoner of myself? O you poor, wretched fellow, have you taken a wife? Fie, fie upon such wretchedness and bitterness! It is better to remain free and lead a peaceful, carefree life; I will become a priest or a nun and compel my children to do likewise."
>
> What then does Christian faith say to this? It opens its eyes, looks upon all these insignificant, distasteful, and despised duties in the Spirit, and is aware that they are all adorned with divine approval as with the costliest gold and jewels.

The new eyes of faith also help overcome the war of the sexes by viewing man and woman as what they really are: Both are pleasing to God because he created them both in their bodily specificity (AE 45:17-18):

> From [Gen. 1:27] we may be assured that God divided mankind into two classes, namely, male and female, or a he and a she. This was so pleasing to him that he himself called it a good creation [Gen. 1:31]. Therefore, each one of us must have the kind of body God has created for us. I cannot make myself a woman, nor can you make yourself a man; we do not have that power. But we are exactly as he created us: I a man and you a woman. Moreover, he wills to have his excellent handiwork honored as his divine creation, and not despised. The man is not to despise or scoff at the woman or her body, nor the woman the man. But each should honor the other's image and body as a divine and good creation that is well-pleasing unto God himself.

Evidently, then as now, unbridled or "liberated" sexual intercourse between men and women does not lead to a higher social status for women, especially when that intercourse is intended to remain "fruitless." In fact, the opposite seems to be true, now as well as then. Only teaching the truth about the creation of male and female as well as about marriage and its purposes from God's Word can do that.

Related to this challenge to marriage is, *fifth, the age-old concern that the married life cannot be afforded.* Taking material worries seriously as the prime destroyer of marriages, Luther put it this way (AE 45:47):

> Finally, we have before us one big, strong objection to answer. Yes, they say, it would be a fine thing to be married, but how will I support myself? I have nothing; take a wife and live on that, etc. Undoubtedly, this is the greatest obstacle to marriage; it is this above all which prevents and breaks up marriage and is the chief excuse for fornication.

Being the "greatest obstacle," Luther identifies it by means of the Ten Commandments as a breaking of the greatest, the First Commandment, that is, as "lack of faith and doubt of God's goodness and truth. … They trust in God as long as they know that they do not need him, and that they are well supplied."

The Christian alternative to this empty, meaningless faith is to follow the crucified Christ at this particular place in life in true faith in God's promises also for this life. This is equally clear from God's Word (AE 45:47-48):

> He who would enter into wedlock as a Christian must not be ashamed of being poor and despised, and doing insignificant work. He should take satisfaction in this: first, that his status and occupation are pleasing to God; second, that God will most certainly provide for him if only he does his job to the best of his ability, and that, if he cannot be a squire or a prince, he is a manservant or a maidservant.

Naturally, when speaking of the perils of poverty in marriage, Luther did not think of the spouses alone. He always had their children in mind—the objection "not able to afford marriage" was for him tantamount to "not able to afford children." Based on Matth. 6:25, 33, Ps. 37:25 and Gen. 1, he responded as follows (AE 45:48-49):

> ...whoever finds himself unsuited to the celibate life should see to it right away that he has something to do and to work at; then let him strike out in God's name and get married. A young man should marry at the age of twenty at the latest, a young woman at fifteen to eighteen; that's when they are still in good health and best suited for marriage. Let God worry about how they and their children are to be fed. God makes children; he will surely also feed them. Should he fail to exalt you and them here on earth, then take satisfaction in the fact that he has granted you a Christian marriage, and know that he will exalt you there; and be thankful to him for his gifts and favors.

Trusting in God's material promises, therefore, is not opposed to working hard for one's family's livelihood. It is opposed to worrying about whether this work succeeds and buys enough bread, as Luther explains further in his comments on Ps. 127:2.[18]

---

[18] Cf. WA 40.3:233-235: "This verse seems to sound as if it prohibits work, against that verse in Moses: 'In the sweat of your brow...' and 'Let him who rules do so with care.' I said that this appears to be contradictory because he pronounces labor, early rising, and taking care of things to be in vain, even though elsewhere idleness and laziness are condemned. Here it is necessary to distinguish faith and works, or spirit and flesh. With the heart you ought to trust in God and invoke God. When you marry, participate in the state, then this well pertains to the outward man, to the flesh, not the spirit, to works, not to faith. There you must labor and exercise the old man so that you get up early, lie down late—in other words, that you exercise care according to the old man as to how you prepare food, govern the state, give laws, provide protection and fortifications. If war is imminent, then see to it that you are well prepared against the enemy, but only according to the external man, that is, so that the soul (*animus*) might be empty and free. For the care ought not to proceed beyond the external man. This is to say that the outward man ought not to be idle and lazy, but attentively ought to carry out the service of laboring, thinking, inventing, and caring as an instrument, so that the hands may work, but the heart may look upward from the labor to God and ought to pray for help. In this way, the external man

While it gains much of the attention today, *homosexuality* had not become very common in Germany back in Luther's day. The reformer, accordingly, describes it as a disorder that was first slowly spreading north from Italy[19] via certain monastic orders but, to date, had not done much damage in Germany. He stated, commenting on Gen. 19:3-4 (AE 3:251):

---

is occupied by labors while the heart or the new man offers prayers instead of cares, saying: 'Lord, I have followed your call and therefore do everything in your name—you rule, etc.'

The consolation is so great that it cannot be described in words ... If the family is disobedient, commend the matter to God and do what you can, then you do both with God's approval: You get up early while you do not get up early. You labor, but you do not labor in vain. According to the old man you will eat the bread of tears, but the heart is tranquil and at rest in hope of divine help and blessing."

[19] Elsewhere, highlighting parallels between the papacy and Islam both of whom do not have a proper understanding of marriage, he commented (AE 46:198, see also AE 54:278): "Since they think lightly of marriage, it serves them right that there are dog-marriages (and would to God they were dog-marriages), indeed, also 'Italian marriages' and 'Florentine brides' among them; and they think these things good. I hear one horrible thing after another about what an open and glorious Sodom Turkey is, and everybody who has looked around a little in Rome and Italy knows very well how God revenges and punishes the forbidden marriage [i.e., homosexuality], so that Sodom and Gommorah, which God overwhelmed in days of old with fire and brimstone [Gen. 19:24], must seem a mere jest and prelude compared with these abominations." In the 15th century, Florence indeed seems to have been an early center of unbridled homosexual activity in its citizenry, including pederasty, cf. M. Rocke, *Forbidden Friendships: Homosexuality and Male Culture in Renaissance Florence* (Oxford: Oxford University Press, 1996). Revisiting the "Italian connection" of homosexuality, Luther noted that the Fifth Lateran Council (1512-1517) dealt with clerics engaging in homosexual acts (cf. AE 47:35-38)—it stripped them of their positions and sent them to a monastery for penance—which he took to mean that it was not an uncommon problem. In 1568, pope Pius V, by his constitution *Horrendum ille scelus*, would go beyond this regulation and hand such clerics over to be put to death by the secular arm, the common punishment laymen had to endure at the time for engaging in such conduct.

> Moses proceeds with a description of a terrible sin. I for my part do not enjoy dealing with this passage, because so far the ears of the Germans are innocent of and uncontaminated by this monstrous depravity; for even though this disgrace, like other sins, has crept in through an ungodly soldier and a lewd merchant, still the rest of the people are unaware of what is being done in secret. The Carthusian monks deserve to be hated because they were the first to bring this terrible pollution into Germany from the monasteries of Italy. Of course, they were trained and educated in such a praiseworthy manner at Rome.

In summary, the confusion and the challenges that exist today when it comes to marriage are nothing new. They have existed in one way or another ever since Adam and Eve fell from God. This is why Luther had to teach, preach, and write to extol marriage. This is why we today have to do the same.

Luther among Contemporary Marriage Counselors: True Beauty Comes from Without

Yet what are we to say today? There is no lack of well-meaning advocates and defenders of marriage among us. And they all show zeal. Yet with Paul one must ask: Is their zeal guided by a proper understanding of God's Word, the human condition after the fall, and marriage itself?

Some years ago, *when it comes to entering marriage*, it was popular in some Christian circles in the US to give out "purity" or "chastity rings," with financial support from the federal government. This practice was coupled with the signing of virginity pledges. From a biblical perspective, this, while certainly well-intentioned, is a practice that must ultimately fail, as Luther rediscovered in the 16th century: Then as now, if there is no special gift from God involved, no amount of rings, vows, pledges, or government or church dollars can or will keep a young person chaste outside of marriage. The divinely given desire to procreate—often disguised by sin as a desire to have "just" sexual intercourse—is too powerful for humans to control.

Other advocates of abstinence, such as Pam Stenzel, a Minnesota-based abstinence-only educator and speaker who has appeared on national radio and TV programs,[20] have developed a number of candid talks and entire programs that drive home the message: Abstinence keeps you pure for your future spouse and saves your life. Promiscuity leads to all kinds of sexually transmitted diseases and depletes those hormones that enable you to bond permanently. Here again, the intention is good and the individual elements are mostly valid, but an almost exclusive focus on the threats of the law, without the gospel and, particularly, the offer of the remedy that marriage is by God's design, will prove equally futile: Already in Luther's day, breaking the traditional vows of chastity was considered a sacrilege that was said to have serious consequences (such as excommunication)—to no avail.

In other words, at a time when children are often seen as a "choice" that gets in the way of other options that are presented and embraced as more rewarding in one way or another—such as a career or a post-high school education—marriage is often put off as well. By way of consequence, young men and women, with their sexual urges in full bloom, engage in the life of "singles." In most cases, the life of a "single" will mean the sexually active, uncommitted adult, not the "unmarried" person Paul was writing about in 1 Cor. 7. For to the latter the apostle wrote that, if he could not exercise self-control in sexual matters, he should get married, whereby he would enter the divine institution of marriage to beget and raise children in a God-pleasing manner.

As an aside, if, as seen above, the wife is the *husband's* helper

[20] Http://pamstenzel.com/MeetPam.aspx.

when it comes to the begetting of offspring,[21] husbands need to play a central role when it comes to children and their Christian upbringing:[22] Children are primarily their business, and, one could say, they are their primary business. In other words, when careers or education are criticized as valid reasons against (entering into marriage and then also having) children, one should not exclusively look to the wife to sacrifice it all for the sake of the husband's ability to live a life of unencumbered professional progress away from his domestic responsibilities. Paternal absenteeism is not a Christian virtue, but a sinful cultural pattern of the West Christians should not emulate. At the end of the day, the parents' careers and education serve the purpose of providing for their children (cf. 2 Cor. 12:14) who, in turn, have a responsibility to provide for their parents (cf. Matth. 15:4-6; 1 Tim. 5:4, 8).

When it comes to offering *counsel to those already in marriage*, variations of the adage "true beauty comes from within" seem

---

[21] Cf. Gen. 2:18. The wife as helper toward offspring is decidedly different from helper toward career or helper toward sexual fulfillment. One of the most popular novels of recent years, Dan Brown's 2003 *The Da Vinci Code*, popularized the notion of the *hieros gamos*. This term, which means holy marriage in Greek, is not there presented as the holy matrimony of the Christian faith, but as sexual intercourse and ecstasy as the most sublime path toward experiencing the deity. Certainly, regardless of Brown's inaccuracies, he seems to have hit a nerve with Western readers where sexual self-help books abound and where a fulfilled sexual life—with marriage or without—is seen as a prerequisite of true happiness in life. Ever mindful of the tremendous impact of the fall on all aspects of human life, Luther, on the other hand, found sexual intercourse after the fall, even though it is still instrumental in the begetting of children as God's greatest work, to be more akin to epilepsy, cf. AE 1:119.

[22] Cf. LC I, 168: "Parents should consider that they owe obedience to God, and that, above all, they should earnestly and faithfully discharge the duties of their office, not only to provide for the material support of their children, servants, subjects, etc., but especially to bring them up to the praise and honor of God."

to abound. There is not only the pop-cultural version of this motto which encourages people to work on their character, or to strive to love and accept themselves, in order to become truly beautiful from within and thus garner the respect and love of others.[23] There is also the Christian variant of this maxim, which ultimately simply replaces the moral code leading to true inner beauty and ability to be loved: Do the right thing according to God's Word and your marriage will be great.

One of the Christian representatives of this approach is Emerson Eggerichs, founder of Michigan-based *Love and Respect Ministries* and internationally known public speaker on male-female relationships.[24] Drawing heavily on Eph. 5, a text also important for Luther's way of counseling married couples, he develops from it what he, also based on psychological research, considers to be the two basic requirements for a successful marriage: Husbands must love their wives, thereby satisfying their greatest desire. Wives must respect their husbands, thereby satisfying their greatest need.[25]

While the concrete steps of such an approach have merit insofar as they are based on God's Word, what is lacking is the great biblical rediscovery of Luther which he expounds in great detail in the two sermons contained in this little volume: The true beauty of marriage and in marriage comes as a gift from without, from the outside of man, not as a result of man's (pious) efforts, from within, from the inside of man. In other words, what is missing is the proper theological framework from which alone individual acts of marital love can be sustained over the period of a life-long marriage.

In other words, Luther does not start by telling spouses: If

---

[23] Cf., e.g., http://thedailylove.com/true-beauty-comes-from-within/.

[24] Http://loveandrespect.com/about-us/.

[25] Cf. E. Eggerichs, *Love & Respect: The Love She Most Desires, the Respect He Desperately Needs* (Nashville, TN: Th. Nelson, 2004).

you want to improve and save your marriage, you must do this, that, or the other thing. While there is a wealth of this kind of advice found in Luther as well, he first lays the foundation by inculcating the simple fact that marriage in general is an institution and the particular spouses are clothed beautifully in God's own Word:[26] Not only is marriage established by God in paradise, which makes living in it highly pleasing to God. It has also been used by God to provide a picture of Christ's union to his bride, the Church (Eph. 5). Moreover, these two spouses joined together in marriage have also been given to one another by God and therefore been made beautiful *for one another* beyond compare. This true beauty, perceived only by the eyes of faith in God's Word, is not only sublime. It is also indestructible by the failings of the spouses.

---

[26] The analogy is baptism's water and one's parents and other authorities, as Luther stated in the Large Catechism (IV, 19-20): "Therefore, we constantly teach that the sacraments and all the external things ordained and instituted by God should be regarded not according to the gross, external mask (as we see the shell of a nut) but as that in which God's Word is enclosed. In the same way we speak about the parental estate and civil authority. If we regard these persons with reference to their noses, eyes, skin and hair, flesh and bones, they look no different from Turks and heathen. Someone might come and say, 'Why should I think more of this person than of others?' But because the commandment is added, 'You shall honor father and mother,' I see another man, adorned and clothed with the majesty and glory of God. *The commandment, I say, is the golden chain about his neck, yes, the crown on his head, which shows me how and why I should honor this particular flesh and blood.*" See also LC I, 108: "Young people must therefore be taught to revere their parents as God's representatives, and to remember that, however lowly, poor, feeble, and eccentric they may be, they are their own father and mother, given them by God. They are not to be deprived of their honor because of their ways or their failings. *Therefore, we are not to think of their persons, whatever they are, but of the will of God, who has created and ordained them to be our parents.* In other respects, indeed, we are all equal in the sight of God, but among ourselves there must be this sort of inequality and proper distinctions. God therefore commands you to be careful to obey me as your father and to acknowledge my authority."

This is what Luther wants to be driven home, and believed, above all: Marriage is pleasing to God, and living with this particular spouse of mine is pleasing to God, despite all adversity we might face together but also despite all the quirkiness or even hostility I might encounter from my spouse. Once this is believed, the necessary hard work of increasing mutual love and respect will commence in earnest for as long as both spouses shall live. If this is not believed, even the best efforts on part of the spouses alone will lack the proper motivation and will eventually run out of steam, especially if they remain unrequited over a period of time.

Drawing on thesis 28 of Luther's 1518 Heidelberg Disputation,[27] one might call the "true beauty from within" approach as that typical of human love that requires a lovable object to come into existence, while the "true beauty from without" approach is typical of preceding divine love as it first makes its object lovable.

About the Text of the Sermons

The first of the two sermons contained in this edition, the one on Hebr. 13, was preached by Luther in 1531, probably on January 8 of that year. It is no longer known whose wedding service it was. This version appeared in a few prints during that year and found its way into the collected works editions, beginning with volume five of the Jena Edition (1557). The 19th-century St. Louis Edition reprinted the text in modernized German in volume 12, col. 1984-1999. A second, slightly modified edition of this sermon appeared in 1536 when it was printed together with the second sermon contained in this edition, the one on

[27] Cf. AE 31:41: "The love of God does not find, but creates, that which is pleasing to it. The love of man comes into being through that which is pleasing to it."

Eph. 5.[28] The 1536 edition of the text is also found in the historic collected works editions, beginning with volume four of the Wittenberg Edition (1551). In the St. Louis Edition, the 1536 version of the sermon is reprinted, again in modernized German, in volume 12, col. 2000-2017.[29] This text from this edition is the basis for the translation contained in this edition.

The second of the two sermons was preached by Luther on April 24, 1536, the Monday after the Second Sunday of Easter (*Quasimodogeniti*),[30] at Eilenburg castle in electoral Saxony during a service in which Caspar Cruciger (1504-1548) was married to his second wife, Apollonia Gunterode of Leipzig, after his first wife, Elizabeth the hymn writer, had died in the previous year. Its only 16th-century print outside the collected works editions took place in the same year, when it was published in a small booklet together with the abovementioned sermon on Hebr. 13. The St. Louis Edition contains the text of the 1536 print in a modernized German version in volume 12, col. 2018-2031.[31] This text of the St. Louis Edition is, once again, the basis for the translation offered here.

To my knowledge, this is the first English translation of these sermons. However, they will also be included in the extension of the American Edition of Luther's Works, currently undertaken by Concordia Publishing House, St. Louis. As of this writing, the respective volumes have not been published.[32]

---

[28] M. Luther, *Zwo Hochzeit Predigten* (Wittenberg: H. Lufft, 1536).

[29] Cf. the editorial remarks in WA 34.2:581-583. Cf. WA 34.1:50-75 for a side-by-side print of both the 1531 and 1536 versions of the sermon.

[30] Luther referred to the traditional gospel lesson of that Sunday, John 20:19-29, in this sermon.

[31] Cf. the editorial remarks in WA 41:XXXII. Cf. WA 41:547-563 for the reprint of G. Rörer's sermon notes above the 1536 printed text.

[32] Cf. http://www.cph.org/images/topics/pdf/luthersworks/Prospectus.pdf, texts 7.55 (p. 25) and 7.83 (p. 26).

The 1536 print combining these two sermons provided the idea for this edition. Once again we seek to make Luther's biblical teaching better known today by translating works that, already in the 16th century, were made available in print to a relatively broad readership. The ultimate goal is still the same, to provide readers with clear, reliable instruction in the Christian faith and all its articles.

The Translator

Lutheran Press

is a non-profit corporation established to publish and promote the theology of Martin Luther. Although many of Luther's works are already available to the general public, their publication as part of collected works editions has prevented them from being widely disseminated. Of special interest to Lutheran Press are the smaller topical works of Luther that continue to address the Christian Church today, but nonetheless, remain effectively unknown. The mission of Lutheran Press is to make such works available on the internet free of charge and by mail at a minimal cost, with proceeds used to publish additional works.

To learn more about Lutheran Press or to order any of our books please contact us at:

Lutheran Press, Inc.
7835 Monroe Street NE
Minneapolis, MN 55432

Lutheran Press
Minneapolis

www.lutheranpress.com

THE BLESSING OVER BRIDEGROOM AND BRIDE BEFORE THE ALTAR

Thus writes Moses in Genesis 2:

And God the Lord said: It is not good for man to be alone. I will make a helper for him to stand by him. Then God the Lord let a deep sleep fall over man, and he fell asleep. And he took one of his ribs and closed the place with flesh. And God the Lord built a woman from the rib which he had taken from man and brought her to him. Then man said: This is bone of my bone and flesh of my flesh. She will be called woman because she was taken from man. Therefore a man will leave his father and his mother and cling to his wife, and they will be one flesh.

Prayer

Lord God, you have created man and woman and ordained them for the institution of marriage. You have also blessed them with the fruits of the body, and have signified by this institution of marriage the sacrament of your dear Son Jesus Christ and the church, his bride. We pray your boundless goodness that you would not allow such creature, ordinance, and blessing of yours to be changed or corrupted but that you would graciously preserve it among us, through Jesus Christ, our Lord. Amen.